Taco Fiesta: A Journey Through Tacos

Discover the Art of Taco Making with Over 100 Irresistible Recipes

VIRGINIA RUSSELL

TABLE OF CONTENTS

TABLE OF CONTENTS...3

INTRODUCTION...8

1. Leftover Chicken Tacos....................................10

2. Slow Cooker Chicken Tacos................................12

3. Citrus and Herb Chicken Taco............................14

4. Creamy Chicken & avocado tacos.........................17

5. Chicken corn tacos with Olives...........................19

6. Chicken chili Verde tacos.................................21

7. Chicken Cheddar Charred Corn tacos...................23

8. Chicken tacos with rice and Sherry......................25

9. Grilled chicken & red pepper taco.......................27

10. Beef Tacos...30

11. Beef Wild Mushroom, Steak, and Poblano Tacos...32

12. Low Fat Beef & Bean Tacos.............................34

13. Beef Cheddar Tacos.....................................36

14. Slow Cooker Chicken Tacos............................38

15. Quick and Easy Ground Turkey Tacos.................40

16. Slow Cooker Cilantro Lime Chicken Tacos...........42

17. Chicken Tacos with Homemade Salsa..................44

18. Lime Chicken Soft Tacos................................46

19. Tex Mex Chicken Tacos.................................48

20. Chicken Tacos on Hard Shells & Refried Beans....50

21. Apple and Onion Chicken Soft Tacos..................52

22. Fajita Chicken Tacos.................................54

23. Fiesta Chicken Tacos.................................56

24. Grilled Chicken Tacos...............................58

25. Soft Chicken and Corn Tacos.......................60

26. Rotisserie Chicken Cheddar Taco..................62

27. Buffalo Chicken Tacos...............................64

28. BBQ beef tacos.......................................66

29. Tacos De Barbacoa...................................68

30. Crispy Venison Tacos................................70

31. Carne Asada Steak Tacos...........................72

32. Chickpea Crepe Tacos with Veal and Eggplant.....74

33. Steak Tacos and Salsa..............................77

34. Ground Beef Tacos...................................79

35. Pan Tacos with Ground Beef and White Rice.........81

36. Tacos with Leftover Hamburgers....................83

37. Buffalo-Style Beef Tacos............................85

38. Beef Taco Wraps.....................................87

39. Carnitas-Style Grilled Beef Tacos...................89

40. Tiny Taco Beef Tarts.................................92

41. One Pot Cheesy Taco Skillet........................94

42. Skirt Steak Street Tacos............................96

43. Puerto Rican Taco....................................99

44. Meaty Taco Casserole..............................101

45. Beef Cilantro Taco..................................103

46. Tomato Soup beef tacos............................106

47. Grilled lamb with soft tacos........................108

48. Grilled pork tacos & papaya salsa..................110

49. Shredded Pork Tacos................................112

50. Pork and Eggs Taco................................114

51. Pork Carnitas Tacos...............................116

52. Taco Truck Tacos..................................118

53. Tacos with Grilled Kielbasa.......................120

54. Picadillo tacos...................................123

55. Pork tacos, California style......................126

56. Honey-Cilantro Shrimp Soft Tacos..................129

57. Baja Fish Tacos...................................131

58. Shrimp Tacos.....................................133

59. Fish Tacos with Cilantro Slaw and Chipotle Mayo
....135

60. Grilled Shrimp and Black Bean Tacos...............137

61. Blackened Cabo Fish Tacos.........................139

62. Spicy Shrimp Tacos...............................141

63. Tilapia Tacos....................................143

64. Mojito-Grilled Fish Tacos with Lime Slaw Topping
....145

65. Grilled fish tacos with cilantro sauce............147

66. Healthy Fish Tacos...............................149

67. Cajun shrimp tacos with tomatillo salsa...........151

68. Ceviche tacos....................................154

69. Grilled fish tacos with green salsa...............157

70. Margarita shrimp tacos...........................160

71. Salmon tacos.....................................163

72. Seafood tacos with corn salsa..............................165

73. Soft tacos with red snapper..............................168

74. Fresh Fruit Tacos..............................170

75. Fruit filled low-fat cocoa tacos..............................173

76. Coconut Fruit tacos..............................176

77. Fried pineapple & orange tacos with grated chocolate..............................178

78. Kid's fish taco's..............................181

79. Ice cream tacos..............................183

80. Crunchy Chickpea Tacos..............................185

81. Tempeh tacos..............................187

82. Mushroom Tacos with Chipotle Cream..............................189

83. Lentil, Kale & Quinoa Tacos..............................191

84. Corn Salsa Topped Black Bean Tacos..............................193

85. Grilled Haloumi Tacos..............................196

86. The Simple Vegan Taco..............................198

87. Beans and Grilled Corn Taco..............................200

88. Black Beans and Rice Salad Taco..............................202

89. Chewy Walnut Tacos..............................204

90. Seitan Tacos..............................206

91. Terrific tofu tacos..............................208

92. Rajas con Crema Tacos..............................210

93. Sweet Potato and Carrot Tinga Tacos..............................212

94. Potato and Chorizo Tacos..............................214

95. Summer Calabacitas Tacos..............................216

96. Spicy Zucchini and Black Bean Tacos..............................218

97. Asparagus tacos...221

98. Bean sprouts taco with beef.........................223

99. Guacamole bean tacos..............................224

100. Lentil tacos...226

CONCLUSION.......................................228

INTRODUCTION

Welcome to "Taco Fiesta: A Culinary Journey Through Flavorful Tacos"! This cookbook is a celebration of the beloved Mexican dish that has captured the hearts and taste buds of food enthusiasts worldwide. Get ready to embark on a tantalizing adventure as we explore the diverse world of tacos, from traditional classics to innovative fusion creations.

In this cookbook, we have curated a collection of over 100 irresistible taco recipes that will take your taste buds on a thrilling rollercoaster ride. From sizzling street-style tacos to gourmet twists and vegetarian delights, each recipe is meticulously crafted to bring out the vibrant flavors, textures, and aromas that make tacos truly exceptional.

Whether you're a seasoned chef or a kitchen novice, this cookbook is designed to inspire and guide you through the art of taco making. Each recipe is accompanied by clear instructions, helpful tips, and vibrant photographs that will entice your senses and make your culinary journey all the more delightful.

So, grab your apron, stock up on tortillas, and let "Taco Fiesta" be your guide to creating unforgettable taco feasts for family and friends. Get ready to elevate your taco game and infuse your meals with a fiesta of flavors. Let's dive into the world of tacos and embark on a culinary adventure like no other!

1. Leftover Chicken Tacos

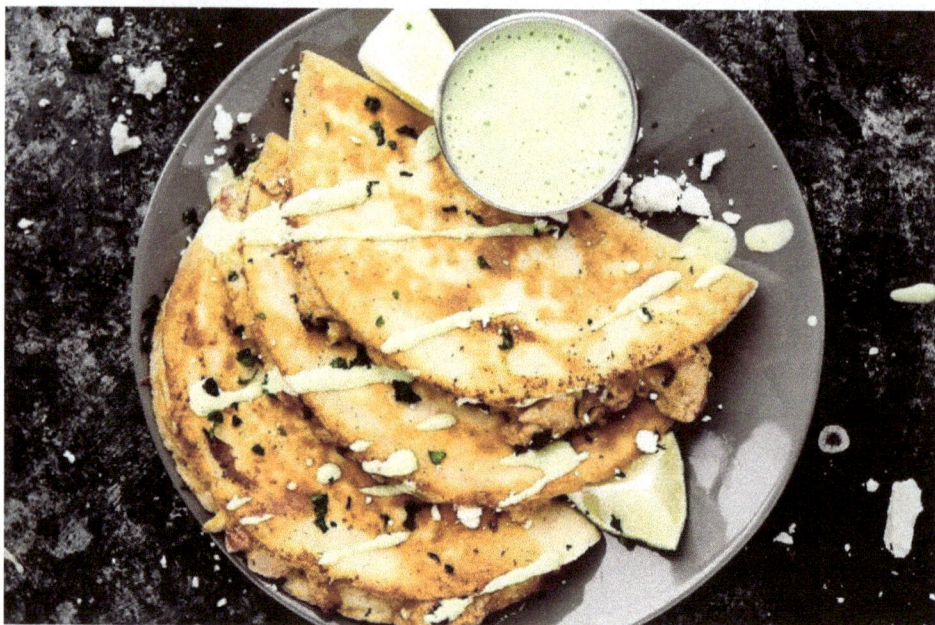

Makes: 2

INGREDIENTS:
- 2 cups of cooked, shredded chicken
- 1 cup tomatillo salsa
- 2 tablespoons oil
- 1 garlic clove, pressed
- 500 grams black beans, cooked and drained
- $\frac{1}{4}$ teaspoon salt
- 4 tortillas
- 1 avocado, sliced

INSTRUCTIONS:
a) Discard the chicken skin by pulling the meat from it.

b) In a large skillet, over medium-low heat, warm the salsa and chicken.

c) Meanwhile, in a medium skillet, heat oil and cook garlic and beans.

d) Add salt and $\frac{1}{2}$-cup water. Crush the beans with the back of the spoon to get a creamy mixture. Remove from heat.

e) Warm the tortillas then add chicken, and top with avocados, salsa, cilantro, lime wedges and your refried beans mixture.

2. <u>Slow Cooker Chicken Tacos</u>

INGREDIENTS:
- 2 pounds chicken breast or thighs
- 8 pieces organic or regular tortillas
- 1 cup organic or homemade salsa
- $\frac{1}{2}$ cup water
- 2 teaspoon ground cumin
- 2 teaspoon chili powder
- 1 teaspoon garlic powder
- 1 teaspoon ground coriander
- $\frac{1}{4}$ teaspoon cayenne pepper (more for more heat)
- $\frac{1}{2}$ teaspoon sea salt
- $\frac{1}{4}$ teaspoon black pepper
- Toppings: Fresh chopped veggies of choice, fresh cilantro, olives, avocado, fresh salsa, lime wedge etc.

INSTRUCTIONS:
a) Put chicken pieces in slow cooker along with water, ground cumin, chili powder, garlic powder, ground coriander, cayenne pepper, salt, and pepper. Mix to coat the chicken.

b) Cook for 4 to 5 hours on high.

c) Remove the chicken and shred. Return to slow cooker and cook for another 30 minutes.

d) Serve chicken in tortilla wraps and add salsa and toppings of your choice.

3. Citrus and Herb Chicken Taco

Makes: 12 Tacos

INGREDIENTS:
TACOS
- 6 Chicken Thighs, with skin
- 3 Chicken Breasts, with skin
- 2 Limes, zest and juice
- 2 Lemons, zest and juice
- 1 cup Mixed fresh herbs
- $\frac{1}{4}$ cup Vermouth or dry white wine
- $\frac{1}{4}$ cup Olive Oil
- 1 teaspoon Cumin, toasted
- 1 teaspoon Coriander, toasted
- 1 teaspoon Garlic, minced

GARNISH IDEAS:
- Picked Cilantro Lime wedges Radish matchsticks
- Lettuce julienned (spinach, ice berg, butter, or cabbage)
- Pico de Gallo
- Shredded Cheese
- Sour Cream
- Pickled hot peppers

TO ASSEMBLE
- 12 flour tortillas

INSTRUCTIONS:
TACOS
a) Combine all the ingredients and let the chicken marinate for at least 4 hours.

b) Grill the chicken, skin side down on the grill first.

c) When cool enough to handle chop roughly.

TO ASSEMBLE THE TACOS

a) Take two tortillas and put about a ¼ or chicken in each and top with desired garnishes.

b) Serve black bean and rice salad alongside tacos.

4. Creamy Chicken & avocado tacos

Makes: 1 serving

INGREDIENTS:
- 1 ounce ripe avocado
- 2 tablespoons Low fat natural yogurt
- 1 teaspoon Lemon juice
- Salt and pepper
- Few lettuce leaves shredded
- 1 Shallot or 3 spring onions, Trimmed and sliced.
- 1 Tomato cut into wedges
- Quarter of a Pepper, finely chopped
- 2 Taco shells
- 2 ounces roast chicken, sliced

INSTRUCTIONS:
a) In a small bowl mash, the avocado with a fork until smooth. Add the yogurt and lemon juice and stir until blended. Season with salt and pepper.

b) Mix together the lettuce, shallot or spring onions, tomato and green or red pepper.

c) Warm the taco shells under a moderate grill for 2 to 3 minutes.

d) Remove them and fill with the salad mixture. Top with the chicken and spoon over the avocado dressing. Serve immediately.

5. <u>Chicken corn tacos with Olives</u>

Makes: 1 serving

INGREDIENTS:

- ⅔ cup Plus 2 Tbs. cooked chicken breast; shredded
- 1 pack Taco seasoning mix
- 3 ounces Canned Mexican style corn; drained
- 4 Taco shells or flour tortillas
- ⅓ cup Plus 1 Tbs. lettuce; shredded
- ½ medium Tomato; chopped
- 1 tablespoon Plus 2 teaspoon sliced ripe olives
- 1 ounce Shredded cheddar cheese

INSTRUCTIONS:

a) Combine chicken and taco seasoning mix in a skillet over medium high heat.

b) Add the amount of water directed on package for taco filling. Bring to a boil. Reduce heat to medium.

c) Simmer 5-10 minutes, stirring occasionally, or until water is evaporated. Stir in corn and cook until thoroughly heated.

d) Meanwhile, heat taco shells or tortillas as directed on package. Fill each shell with ¼ cup chicken filling.

e) Top each with lettuce, tomato, olives and cheese.

6. Chicken chili Verde tacos

Makes: 4 servings

INGREDIENTS:
- 3 cups Shredded cabbage
- 1 cup Fresh cilantro -- lightly Packed
- 1 cup Green chili salsa
- 1 pounds Boneless skinless chicken Breasts
- 1 teaspoon Salad oil
- 1 Boneless skinless chicken Breasts -- slivered Lengthwise
- 3 Cloves garlic -- minced
- 1 teaspoon Ground cumin
- $\frac{1}{2}$ teaspoon Dried oregano
- 8 Flour tortillas
- Reduced fat or regular

INSTRUCTIONS:
a) Combine cabbage, cilantro, and salsa in a serving dish; set aside.

b) Cut chicken crosswise into $\frac{1}{2}$-inch wide strips. In a 10 to 12 inch nonstick frying pan over medium-high heat, stir oil, onion, and garlic for 2 minutes. Increase heat to high, add chicken, and stir often until meat is no longer pink in center, 4 to 6 minutes.

c) Add cumin and oregano; stir for 15 seconds. Spoon into serving dish. 3.

d) Wrap tortillas in a cloth towel and cook in microwave oven on full power until hot, about $1\frac{1}{2}$ minutes. At the table, spoon the cabbage and chicken mixtures into the tortillas.

7. Chicken Cheddar Charred Corn tacos

Makes: 1 serving

INGREDIENTS:

- ⅔ cup Plus 2 Tbs. cooked chicken breast; shredded
- 1 pack Taco seasoning mix
- 3 ounces Charred Corn
- 4 Taco shells or flour tortillas
- ⅓ cup Plus 1 Tbs. lettuce; shredded
- ½ medium Tomato; chopped
- 1 tablespoon Plus 2 teaspoon sliced ripe olives
- Sour cream
- 1 ounce Shredded cheddar cheese

INSTRUCTIONS:

a) Combine chicken and taco seasoning mix in a skillet over medium high heat.

b) Add the amount of water directed on package for taco filling. Bring to a boil.

c) Reduce heat to medium. Simmer 5-10 minutes, stirring occasionally, or until water is evaporated.

d) Stir in corn and cook until thoroughly heated.

e) Meanwhile, heat taco shells or tortillas as directed on package. Fill each shell with ¼ cup chicken filling.

f) Top each with lettuce, tomato, olives and cheese.

g) Drizzle sour cream on top.

8. Chicken tacos with rice and Sherry

Makes: 6 servings

INGREDIENTS:
- 2 pounds Chicken parts
- $\frac{1}{4}$ cup Flour
- 2 teaspoons Salt
- $\frac{1}{4}$ teaspoon Pepper
- 1 cup Onion, chopped
- $\frac{1}{4}$ cup Butter
- 2 tablespoons Worcestershire sauce
- $\frac{1}{4}$ teaspoon Garlic powder
- 1 cup Chili sauce
- $1\frac{1}{2}$ cup Chicken broth
- 3 cups Hot Rice, cooked
- $\frac{1}{2}$ cup Dry Sherry

INSTRUCTIONS:
a) Roll chicken in combined flour, salt, and pepper.
b) Brown in Margarine.
c) Push chicken to one side.
d) Add onions, sauté until transparent.
e) Stir in remaining ingredients except rice. Bring to a boil, cover and reduce heat, then simmer for 35 minutes.
f) Serve chicken and sauce over bed of fluffy rice.

9. <u>Grilled chicken & red pepper taco</u>

Makes: 6 Servings

INGREDIENTS:

- 1½ pounds Boneless, skinless chicken b
- 2 Red bell peppers roasted pee
- 2 Stalks celery, washed and sliced
- 1 Med red onion, peeled and chopped
- ½ cup Cooked black beans
- ¼ cup Chopped cilantro leaves
- ¼ cup Balsamic vinegar
- ¼ cup Oil
- ¼ cup Orange juice
- ¼ cup Lime juice
- 2 Cloves garlic, peeled and mi
- 1 teaspoon Ground coriander seed
- ½ teaspoon Pepper
- ½ teaspoon Salt
- ¼ cup Sour cream or non-fat yogurt
- 6 (8-in) flour tortillas

INSTRUCTIONS:

a) LIGHT A GRILL OR PREHEAT a broiler. Pound the chicken breasts to an even thickness, and grill or broil on both sides until cooked through, but not dried out, about 4 minutes on a side. It Makes: sense to grill the peppers at the same time. Slice, and set aside.

b) Combine the bell peppers, celery, onion, black beans and cilantro in a mixing bowl. Combine the vinegar, oil, orange juice, lime juice, garlic, coriander, pepper. Combine with salt and sour cream or yogurt in a jar with a tight-fitting lid. Shake well, and pour the dressing over the vegetables.

c) Marinate the vegetables for 1 hour at room temperature. Place a large skillet over medium heat, and grill the tortillas for 30 seconds on a side to soften. To serve, divide the chicken among the tortillas, placing it at the center of the tortilla.

d) Divide the vegetables and their dressing on top of the chicken, and roll the tortilla into a cylinder.

e) Serve immediately; the dish should be at room temperature.

10. Beef Tacos

Makes: 8 servings

INGREDIENTS:

- $\frac{1}{2}$ pound lean ground beef
- 8 whole wheat tortillas
- 1 pack taco seasoning
- Shredded romaine lettuce & 2 large tomatoes
- $\frac{3}{4}$ cup water
- 2 cups shredded cheddar cheese

INSTRUCTIONS:

a) Into a medium pan add some water, ground beef, and taco seasoning, then bring everything to a boil.

b) Heat up the tacos on both sides according to the package instructions, then top with the meat, veggies, and sauce.

11. Beef Wild Mushroom, Steak, and Poblano Tacos

Makes: 6 servings

INGREDIENTS:
- 1 tablespoon olive oil
- 12 corn tortillas
- 1 pound beef steak
- 12 tablespoons salsa sauce & $\frac{1}{2}$ teaspoon coriander
- $\frac{1}{2}$ teaspoon salt & black pepper
- 2 cups raw onion & 1 cup minced garlic
- $\frac{3}{4}$ cup Mexican cheese
- 1 Poblano pepper
- 2 cups wild mushrooms

INSTRUCTIONS:
a) Start browning the steak beef meat into an oiled medium pan, together with salt and pepper seasonings. After cooking for 5 minutes on both sides, take out the steaks and set them aside.

b) Add the remaining ingredients into the pan and sauté them for 5 minutes.

c) Serve the warm tortillas topped with the mushroom mixture, sliced steak meat, salsa sauce and shredded Mexican cheese.

12. Low Fat Beef & Bean Tacos

Makes: 4 servings

INGREDIENTS:
- 1 pound ground beef
- refried beans
- 8 taco shells & taco seasoning
- 1 sweet onion
- salsa sauce
- shredded cheddar cheese
- 1 sliced avocado
- sour cream

INSTRUCTIONS:
a) Start cooking the beef into an oiled pan and add the beans and seasonings.

b) Place the tacos onto a plate and add the meat mixture, salsa sauce, sour cream, sliced avocado and shredded cheddar cheese.

13. Beef Cheddar Tacos

Makes: 16 servings

INGREDIENTS:
- 1 ½ pounds lean ground beef
- 8 whole corn tortillas
- 1 pack taco seasoning
- 1 jar salsa sauce
- 2 cups grated cheddar cheese

INSTRUCTIONS:
a) In an oiled frying pan slowly brown the ground beef, add the salsa sauce and mix well, then drain the meat.
b) Warm up each tortilla and add the meat mixture, seasonings, add some salsa sauce and cheddar cheese.

14. <u>Slow Cooker Chicken Tacos</u>

Makes: 8 servings

INGREDIENTS:
- 1 lb chicken breasts
- 1 pack taco seasoning
- 1 jar salsa
- 2-3 tomatoes
- Cheddar cheese

INSTRUCTIONS:
a) Take a medium crock pot and cook the chicken meat for about 8 hours over low heat.
b) Before serving it on tortillas, shred it and add the rest of the ingredients and seasonings.

15. <u>Quick and Easy Ground Turkey Tacos</u>

Makes: 8 servings

INGREDIENTS:

- 1 pound ground turkey
- taco seasonings
- 1 cup shredded cheese
- $\frac{3}{4}$ cup water
- 1 can diced tomatoes with basil, oregano, and garlic
- 1 can black beans
- low carb tortillas & lettuce

INSTRUCTIONS:

a) Into a medium skillet start frying the turkey meat until it gets brown.

b) Add the water, diced tomatoes and beans, simmering until they get consistent.

c) Spoon the mixture over each tortilla, adding lettuce and shredded cheese.

16. Slow Cooker Cilantro Lime Chicken Tacos

Makes: 6 servings

INGREDIENTS:
- 1 lb chicken breasts
- 1 jar salsa
- 3 tablespoons fresh cilantro
- 1 pack Taco seasoning
- 1 Lime (juice)
- 6 whole wheat Tortillas

INSTRUCTIONS:
a) Place the chicken meat, taco seasoning, cilantro, lime juice and salsa into a medium slow cooker; cooking for 8-10 hours over low heat (you can do this overnight).

b) When done, shred the meat and place it over your tortillas, adding the toppings to taste (olives, lettuce, onions & other sauces).

17. Chicken Tacos with Homemade Salsa

Makes: 2 servings

INGREDIENTS:
SPICY MEAT:
- 1 chicken breast (cubed)
- 1 garlic clove
- $\frac{1}{2}$ tomato
- $\frac{1}{2}$ teaspoon onion & chili powder
- $\frac{1}{2}$ teaspoon cumin & paprika
- $\frac{1}{2}$ lime (juice)

SALSA:
- $\frac{1}{4}$ cup diced onion
- $\frac{1}{2}$ diced tomato
- 1 pinch of salt
- $\frac{1}{4}$ cup fresh cilantro
- $\frac{1}{2}$ lime juice
- $\frac{1}{2}$ diced avocado
- $\frac{1}{2}$ small Jalapeño pepper

OTHER:
- 4 corn tortillas
- $\frac{1}{4}$ cup mozzarella cheese
- $\frac{1}{2}$ cup lettuce (shredded)

INSTRUCTIONS:
a) Take a medium skillet, add the chicken, spices, garlic and lime juice, cooking everything until just done.

b) Pour the diced tomatoes over the fried chicken.

c) Meanwhile, start mixing the ingredients for salsa sauce. Heat each corn tortilla, add the chicken mixture, lettuce, salsa sauce, and mozzarella.

18. Lime Chicken Soft Tacos

Makes: 10 servings

INGREDIENTS:

- 1 $\frac{1}{2}$ pounds breast meat (cubed)
- 10 Fajita size tortillas
- $\frac{1}{4}$ cup red wine vinegar
- $\frac{1}{4}$ cup salsa sauce
- $\frac{1}{2}$ lime juice
- 1 teaspoon splenda
- $\frac{1}{4}$ cup Monterey Jack cheese (shredded)
- $\frac{1}{2}$ teaspoon salt & ground black pepper
- 1 diced tomato
- $\frac{1}{2}$ cup lettuce (shredded)
- 2 green onions & garlic cloves
- 1 teaspoon dried oregano

INSTRUCTIONS:

a) In a medium saucepan, sauté the chicken breast over medium heat for about 15 minutes.

b) Add some lime juice, green onion, vinegar, oregano and other seasonings, simmering everything well for 5 more minutes.

c) Heat up each fajita tortilla into a large skillet over medium heat on each side.

d) Make each tortilla, adding the chicken meat mixture,

19. Tex Mex Chicken Tacos

Makes: 4 servings

INGREDIENTS:
- 8 corn tortillas
- 1 pound chicken breast (pieces)
- $\frac{1}{2}$ cup sour cream
- $\frac{1}{2}$ cup orange juice
- 1 teaspoon cornstarch
- $\frac{1}{4}$ cup fresh cilantro
- 1 cup frozen whole kernel corn
- 1 teaspoon lime peel
- 1 jalapeno pepper
- 1 medium sweet red pepper
- 3 garlic cloves
- 2 teaspoon olive oil
- $\frac{1}{4}$ teaspoon salt and black pepper

INSTRUCTIONS:
a) Place the chicken meat and other marinade ingredients into a plastic bag and place it into the fridge for 1-2 hours. When it's well marinated, drain it and cook it into a medium frying pan, until crispy and tender.

b) Add the sweet peppers, some marinade and cornstarch and cook everything for 2 minutes more.

c) Heat up each tortilla in your microwave for 40 seconds, divide the chicken among them, and add some sour cream, lettuce, onions, and seasonings.

20. Chicken Tacos on Hard Shells & Refried Beans

Makes: 5 servings

INGREDIENTS:
- 1 cup shredded Mexican cheese
- 5 corn tacos
- 1 pound chicken meat
- 1 pack taco seasonings
- 1 cup chopped onions & tomatoes
- $\frac{3}{4}$ cup water & 1 can refried beans
- 3 ounces Spinach leaves
- $\frac{1}{2}$ cup salsa sauce

INSTRUCTIONS:
a) Start cutting the chicken meat and onions into small pieces, then cook them into a medium skillet over medium heat for 2-3 minutes.

b) Add the spinach leaves, water and seasonings, bring everything to a boil.

c) Warm up each corn tortilla in a microwave oven, add the chicken mixture, some more spinach leaves, tomatoes, refried beans, salsa sauce, cheese and some seasonings.

21. Apple and Onion Chicken Soft Tacos

Makes: 4 servings

INGREDIENTS:
- 6 Flour tortillas
- 2 chicken breasts (cubes)
- 1 tablespoon butter
- 1 garlic clove
- $\frac{1}{2}$ teaspoon ground nutmeg & black pepper
- 2 cups sliced apples & 1 cup sliced onion
- 4 tablespoons mango salsa
- 1 tablespoon olive oil

INSTRUCTIONS:
a) Over medium heat, heat some butter into a medium frying pan.

b) Add the apples and onions, cooking them until they get browned. Take out the apples and onions, and cook the cubed chicken breasts until cooked through.

c) Transfer the onions and apples, minced garlic and seasonings.

d) Top each tortilla with the mixture and some mango salsa.

22. Fajita Chicken Tacos

Makes: 1 serving

INGREDIENTS:
- 1 pound Chicken Meat
- 3 corn tortillas
- $\frac{1}{4}$ can cheddar cheese
- 1 teaspoon fajita seasoning
- $\frac{1}{4}$ can tomatoes
- $\frac{1}{4}$ lettuce
- 1 tablespoon salsa-mild

INSTRUCTIONS:
a) Cook the chunk, chicken, and fajita seasonings.

b) In a medium pan, warm up each corn tortilla, until they get crispy.

c) Place 1 teaspoon of salsa sauce over each tortilla, add the chicken and other vegetables.

23. Fiesta Chicken Tacos

Makes: 10 servings

INGREDIENTS:
- 1 ½ pound chicken breast
- ½ tablespoons onion & garlic powder
- 1 can nacho cheese soup
- 1 pack taco seasoning
- 6 tablespoons green chili sauce
- 4 tablespoons salsa

INSTRUCTIONS:
a) Take a crockpot and add the chicken breast. In a medium bowl, mix the other ingredients and then pour them over the chicken.

b) Set the cooking time to 6-8 hours over low heat. Shred the chicken using a small knife.

24. Grilled Chicken Tacos

INGREDIENTS:

- ½ kg chicken thighs, skinned and deboned
- 1 medium onion, peeled and cut into large wedges
- 2 garlic cloves, finely chopped
- 1 tablespoon cumin seeds, chopped
- 1 tablespoon vegetable oil
- 1 teaspoon salt
- ½ teaspoon black pepper
- 8 tortillas

INSTRUCTIONS:

a) Set the grill at medium-high heat. In a medium bowl, toss chicken, onions, garlic, cumin, salt, pepper and oil.

b) Grill the onion and chicken for four minutes on each side or until it is lightly charred and cooked throughout.

c) Allow the chicken to cool for a few minutes before cutting it to serve with sliced avocados, Charred Tomatillo Salsa Verde, Cilantro sprigs, lime wedges and sliced radishes.

25. <u>Soft Chicken and Corn Tacos</u>

Makes: 5

INGREDIENTS:
- $\frac{1}{2}$ kg boneless chicken, cut into thin strips
- 1 cup Salsa
- 25 grams Taco Seasoning
- 2 cups white rice
- 10 flour tortillas
- $\frac{3}{4}$ cup Shredded Cheese
- Corn kernels
- Shredded cilantro for garnish

INSTRUCTIONS:
a) Over medium-high heat, heat some oil in a large skillet.

b) Add the chicken and stir-fry it for approximately 7 minutes or until the chicken is done.

c) Add 2 cups of water, salsa and seasoning mix and bring the mixture to boil.

d) Add the rice, cover and cook it for 5 minutes.

e) Spoon the mixture onto previously warmed tortillas and sprinkle it generously with the cheddar cheese.

f) Add some corn kernels as desired.

g) Garnish with cilantro.

26. Rotisserie Chicken Cheddar Taco

Makes: 6

INGREDIENTS:
- 3 cups rotisserie chicken, finely chopped or shredded
- ½ cup salsa
- 2 tablespoons honey
- 1 tablespoon lime
- 2 tablespoons Taco seasoning
- Salt
- Pepper
- 6 corn Tortillas
- Olive oil
- Cheddar cheese, shredded

INSTRUCTIONS:
a) Whisk all the ingredients together except the chicken and cheese.

b) Place the shredded chicken in a microwave safe container and stir in the rest of the mixture.

c) Place this container inside the microwave for 2 minutes, take it

d) out, stir and repeat the process until the chicken is properly heated.

e) Sprinkle some oil onto a skillet and warm the tortillas until they are golden-brown in color on both sides.

f) Place the chicken mixture equally on all the tortillas. Sprinkle with shredded cheese and serve with lettuce, quartered cherry

g) tomatoes, cilantro and sour cream.

27. <u>Buffalo Chicken Tacos</u>

Makes: 3

INGREDIENTS:
- 1 cup celery (diced)
- 2 cups rotisserie Chicken, shredded finely
- $\frac{1}{2}$ cup red hot, buffalo wing sauce
- 1 tablespoon oil
- 6 corn tortillas
- 1 $\frac{1}{2}$ cup Mexican cheese (blend)
- Salt

INSTRUCTIONS:
a) Place the shredded chicken in a bowl and pour the Buffalo sauce over it. Mix well then pop it into the microwave to heat it up.

b) Pour one tablespoon of oil on a skillet and, using the tortillas,

c) evenly spread the oil all over. Sprinkle some sea salt over one side

d) of the tortillas as you allow them to turn a golden brown in the

e) process.

f) Within 30 seconds flip each tortilla over and sprinkle the other side with some cheese. You may also use regular cheddar cheese. Once the cheese melts, sprinkle with chicken and celery.

g) Serve with blue cheese sprinkled over the top or some spicy sauce.

28. BBQ beef tacos

Makes: 8 servings

INGREDIENTS:

- 1 pound lean ground beef (or turkey)
- $\frac{1}{2}$ cup Mexican shredded cheese
- 1 sliced onion & red pepper
- 8 whole wheat tortillas
- $\frac{1}{2}$ cup barbecue sauce
- 1 diced tomato

INSTRUCTIONS:

a) Start cooking the beef meat, onions and peppers in a medium oiled skillet until well done, stirring occasionally.

b) Add the sauce and cook everything for 2 minutes.

c) Pour the meat mixture over each tortilla and top with cheese and tomatoes before serving.

29. Tacos De Barbacoa

Makes: 20 servings

INGREDIENTS:

- 4 pounds beef meat
- $\frac{1}{4}$ cup cider vinegar
- 20 corn tortillas
- 3 tablespoons lime juice
- $\frac{3}{4}$ cup chicken broth
- 3-5 canned chipotle chiles
- 2 tablespoons vegetable oil & 3 bay leaves
- 4 garlic cloves & cumin
- 3 teaspoon Mexican oregano
- 1 $\frac{1}{2}$ teaspoon salt & ground black pepper
- $\frac{1}{2}$ teaspoon ground cloves
- onion, cilantro and lime wedges (chopped)

INSTRUCTIONS:

a) Mix into a medium bowl the lime juice, garlic cloves, cider vinegar and other seasonings, until they get smooth like a paste.

b) Take the meat and cook it into an oiled skillet for 5 minutes, over both sides. Add the mixture from the bowl over the meat and keep stirring well.

c) After 10 more minutes, while the ingredients were simmering, add the mixture into the preheated oven. Cook for about 4-5 hours.

d) Serve the corn tortillas with the oven mixture, onions, cilantro, lime wedges and other seasonings.

30. Crispy Venison Tacos

Makes: 7 servings

INGREDIENTS:
- 1 pound ground venison
- 21 taco shells
- 2 tablespoons taco sauce
- 1 can Taco Bell re-fried beans
- 1-2 cups of shredded lettuce
- 1 teaspoon chili seasoning mix
- $1\frac{1}{2}$ cups shredded cheese

INSTRUCTIONS:
a) Start heating up your oven to 325 degrees Celsius and then cook the ground venison into a medium frying pan, until it gets finely browned.

b) Add 2 tablespoons of sauce, seasonings and the re-fried beans, cooking until well warmed through.

c) Meanwhile, warm each tortilla into the oven for a few minutes, and then assemble with lettuce, sauce, meat mixture and some shredded cheese.

31. Carne Asada Steak Tacos

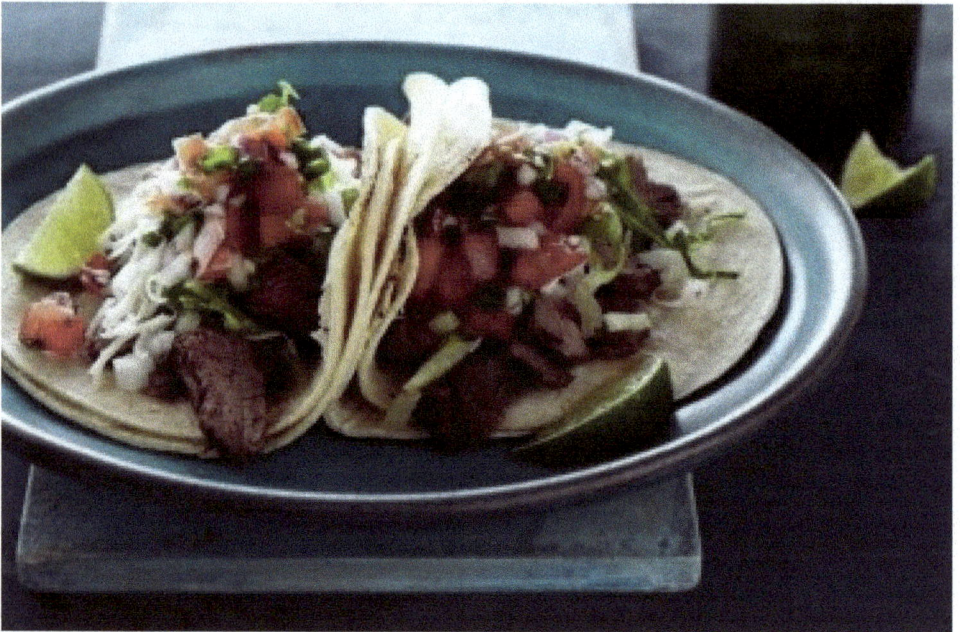

Makes: 12 servings

INGREDIENTS:
- 2 pounds flank steaks

- 1 tablespoon meat seasoning
- 1 lime juiced & 1 teaspoon cumin
- $\frac{1}{2}$ teaspoon salt & ground pepper
- 2 tablespoons minced garlic & 1 dash cayenne pepper
- $\frac{1}{2}$ teaspoon chili powder
- 2 tablespoons fresh cilantro

INSTRUCTIONS:

a) Cut the fat from the meat if needed, then place it into a large bag together with the lime, 2 tablespoons of water, seasonings and place it in the fridge so everything will coat well.

b) Take out the meat and grill it for 5 minutes over each side. Start preparing the tortillas, adding the vegetables, grilled meat, and some seasonings.

32. Chickpea Crepe Tacos with Veal and Eggplant

Makes: 4

INGREDIENTS:
- 2 ¼ cups of chickpea flour
- ¼ cup plain yogurt
- 2 ½ teaspoons salt (divided)
- 3 ½ tablespoons olive oil
- ¼ kg veal (ground)
- 1 ½ teaspoons cumin (ground)
- ¼ teaspoon red pepper flakes (crushed)
- 1 pound eggplant and cut them into cubes 1" in size
- 3 garlic cloves (sliced thinly)
- ¼ cup raisins (golden)
- ¼ cup red wine
- 15 ounce tomatoes (diced)
- ¼ cup pine nuts (toasted)

INSTRUCTIONS:
a) In a medium bowl, whisk the chickpea flour together with the yogurt, 1 ¼ teaspoon salt, and water (2 cups and 1 tablespoon) and set it aside.

b) Over a medium high flame, in a large skillet, heat 1 tablespoon oil. Add the veal, red pepper, cumin and ¼ teaspoon salt to the skillet to cook the veal.

c) Make sure to break and stir the veal often so it does not clump together. As the veal begins to brown, (after about 4 minutes) remove the meat and spices from the skillet and place it in a medium bowl.

d) Heat 2 tablespoons oil on the skillet, before adding eggplant and the remaining salt. Cook the eggplant for 5 minutes or until it turns brown from all sides.

e) Now add garlic and stir occasionally until it turns a light brown color.

f) Add raisins and wine to cook the mixture. Remember to stir continuously, for a minute, so the mixture is heated uniformly.

g) Add the diced tomatoes (with juice), the lamb mixture, pine nuts, and $\frac{1}{4}$

h) cup water. Stir and reduce the heat to medium flame so the mixture

i) can simmer. Stir occasionally. In about 15 minutes, as most of the juices evaporate, close the flame.

j) Swirl the remaining oil in an 8" non-stick skillet, wipe it with a paper towel to leave just a sheen of oil on the skillet, and heat it to medium high.

k) Whisking the flour mixture, pour about a third of a cup into the skillet.

l) Swirl to completely coat the pan with the batter, to make a crepe, cooking both sides until they are browned. Remove the crepe from the skillet and repeat the process with the remaining batter.

m)   Spoon the lamb filling onto the pancakes.

n) Serve with green vegetables, yogurt and lemon wedges.

33. <u>Steak Tacos and Salsa</u>

Makes: 4

INGREDIENTS:
- 2 tablespoons olive oil, divided
- $\frac{1}{2}$ kg flank steak
- Salt
- Black pepper
- $\frac{1}{2}$ cup cilantro leaves
- 4 radishes, trimmed and finely chopped
- 2 spring onions, thinly sliced
- $\frac{1}{2}$ jalapeño, seeds removed and finely chopped
- 2 tablespoons lime juice
- 8 corn tortillas

INSTRUCTIONS:
a) Season the steak with salt and pepper and cook each side in a skillet over high heat.

b) Pour the olive oil in the skillet and cook each side for about 5- 8 minutes. Let it rest for another five minutes.

c) Chop half the cilantro and toss with radishes, jalapenos, onions, lime juice and 1 tablespoon olive oil. Season with salt, pepper and salsa.

d) Slice steak, place on each tortilla along with a portion of the vegetable mixture.

e) Serve with queso fresco cheese and the rest of the cilantro.

34. Ground Beef Tacos

Makes: 4

INGREDIENTS:

- 8 corn tortillas
- 750 grams ground beef
- 4 tablespoons of taco seasoning
- 1 cup iceberg lettuce, shredded
- 1 cup grape tomatoes, halved
- $\frac{1}{2}$ red onion, finely sliced
- 1 avocado, sliced

INSTRUCTIONS:

a) In a skillet, cook ground beef and taco seasoning together, for

b) about 7 minutes on a medium flame so the meat is cooked

c) through. Drain to remove excessive grease.

d) Warm tortillas and assemble using equal portions of beef mixture and top with lettuce, tomatoes, onion and avocados. Serve with lime wedges.

35. Pan Tacos with Ground Beef and White Rice

Makes: 4

INGREDIENTS:
- ½ kg beef
- 1 teaspoon cumin
- 1 tablespoon chilli powder
- 2 cups white rice
- 1 cup cheese, shredded
- 2 cups water
- 8 wheat tortillas
- Salt

INSTRUCTIONS:
a) Brown the meat in a large pan for about 10 minutes. Drain to

b) remove any grease.

c) Add the spices, stir for 30 seconds before adding water. Make sure it is on high heat so it will boil quickly. Stir in the rice and cheese. Cover and allow to simmer on medium heat for 5 minutes.

d) Drain, as needed, to remove extra oil and water.

e) Assemble by placing equal portions on each tortilla, add shredded lettuce, and chopped tomatoes to serve.

36. Tacos with Leftover Hamburgers

Makes: 4

INGREDIENTS:
- 250 grams hamburger
- 1 cup water
- 1 packet taco seasoning
- 8 corn tortillas

INSTRUCTIONS:
a) Add the hamburger (or substitute) to a skillet and heat on medium heat until it is browned, and warmed through.

b) Add the taco seasoning and water and cook for 5 minutes so it is ready to serve.

c) When the meat is thoroughly cooked, assemble tacos using meat and diced vegetables like tomatoes, onions and lettuce. Serve with lime wedges and shredded cheese for topping.

37. Buffalo-Style Beef Tacos

Makes: 4 servings

INGREDIENTS:
- 1-pound Ground Beef (95% lean)
- ¼ cup cayenne pepper sauce for Buffalo wings
- 8 taco shells
- 1 cup thinly sliced lettuce
- ¼ cup reduced fat or regular prepared blue cheese dressing
- ½ cup shredded carrot
- ⅓ cup chopped celery
- 2 tablespoons chopped fresh cilantro
- Carrot and celery sticks or cilantro sprigs

INSTRUCTIONS:
a) Heat large nonstick skillet over medium heat until hot.

b) Add Ground Beef; cook 8 to 10 minutes, breaking into small crumbles and stirring occasionally. Remove from skillet with slotted spoon; pour off drippings.

c) Return to skillet; stir in pepper sauce. Cook and stir 1 minute or until heated through.

d) Meanwhile, heat taco shells according to package instructions.

e) Evenly spoon beef mixture into taco shells. Add lettuce; drizzle with dressing.

f) Top evenly with carrot, celery and cilantro. Garnish with carrot and celery sticks or cilantro sprigs, if desired.

38. <u>Beef Taco Wraps</u>

Makes: 4 servings

INGREDIENTS:
- $\frac{3}{4}$ pound thinly sliced deli roast beef
- $\frac{1}{2}$ cup fat-free black bean dip
- 4 large (about 10-inch diameter) flour tortillas
- 1 cup thinly sliced lettuce
- $\frac{3}{4}$ cup chopped tomato
- 1 cup (4 ounces) shredded reduced-fat taco seasoned cheese
- Salsa

INSTRUCTIONS:
a) Spread black bean dip evenly over one side of each tortilla. Layer deli roast beef over bean dip, leaving $\frac{1}{2}$-inch border around edges.

b) Sprinkle equal amounts of lettuce, tomato and cheese over each tortilla.

c) Fold right and left sides to center, overlapping edges. Fold bottom edge of tortilla up over filling and roll closed.

d) Cut each roll in half. Serve with salsa, if desired.

39. <u>Carnitas-Style Grilled Beef Tacos</u>

Makes: 6 servings

INGREDIENTS:
- 4 beef Flat Iron Steaks (about 8 ounces each)
- 18 small corn tortillas (6 to 7-inch diameter)

TOPPINGS:
- Minced white onion, chopped fresh cilantro, lime wedges

MARINADE:
- 1 cup prepared tomatillo salsa
- ⅓ cup chopped fresh cilantro
- 2 tablespoons fresh lime juice
- 2 teaspoons minced garlic
- ½ teaspoon salt
- ¼ teaspoon pepper
- 1-½ cups prepared tomatillo salsa
- 1 large avocado, diced
- ⅔ cup chopped fresh cilantro
- ½ cup minced white onion
- 1 tablespoon fresh lime juice
- 1 teaspoon minced garlic
- ½ teaspoon salt

INSTRUCTIONS:
a) Combine marinade ingredients in small bowl. Place beef steaks and marinade in food-safe plastic bag; turn steaks to coat. Close bag securely and marinate in refrigerator 15 minutes to 2 hours.

b) Remove steaks from marinade; discard marinade. Place steaks on grid over medium, ash-covered coals. Grill, covered, 10 to 14 minutes for medium rare (145°F) to medium (160°F) doneness, turning occasionally.

c) Meanwhile combine avocado salsa ingredients in medium bowl. Set aside.

d) Place tortillas on grid. Grill until warm and slightly charred. Remove; keep warm.

e) Carve steaks into slices. Serve in tortillas with avocado salsa. Top with onion, cilantro and lime wedges, as desired.

40. Tiny Taco Beef Tarts

Makes: 30 tiny tarts

INGREDIENTS:
- 12 ounces Ground Beef (95% lean)
- $\frac{1}{2}$ cup chopped onion
- 1 clove garlic, finely chopped
- $\frac{1}{2}$ cup prepared mild or medium taco sauce
- $\frac{1}{2}$ teaspoon ground cumin
- $\frac{1}{4}$ teaspoon salt
- $\frac{1}{8}$ teaspoon pepper
- 30 phyllo shells
- $\frac{1}{2}$ cup shredded reduced fat Mexican cheese blend
- Toppings: Shredded lettuce, sliced grape or cherry tomatoes, guacamole, low-fat sour cream, sliced ripe olives

INSTRUCTIONS:
a) Heat oven to 350°F. Heat large nonstick skillet over medium heat until hot.

b) Add Ground Beef, onion and garlic in large nonstick skillet over medium heat 8 to 10 minutes, breaking up beef into small crumbles and stirring occasionally. Pour off drippings, if necessary.

c) Add taco sauce, cumin, salt and pepper; cook and stir 1 to 2 minutes or until mixture is heated through.

d) Place phyllo shells on rimmed baking sheet. Spoon beef mixture evenly into shells. Top evenly with cheese. Bake 9 to 10 minutes or until shells are crisp and cheese is melted.

e) Top tarts with lettuce, tomatoes, guacamole, sour cream, and olives, as desired.

41. <u>One Pot Cheesy Taco Skillet</u>

Makes: 30 tiny tarts

INGREDIENTS:

- 1-pound lean Ground Beef
- 1 large yellow onion, diced
- 2 medium zucchini, diced
- 1 yellow bell pepper, diced
- 1 package taco seasoning
- 1 can diced tomatoes with green chilies
- 1 $\frac{1}{2}$ cup shredded cheddar or Monterey jack cheese
- Green onions for garnish
- Lettuce, rice, flour or corn tortillas for serving

INSTRUCTIONS:

a) Heat large nonstick skillet over medium heat until hot. Add Ground Beef, onion, zucchini and yellow pepper; cook 8 to 10 minutes, breaking into small crumbles and stirring occasionally. Pour off drippings if needed.

b) Add taco seasoning, $\frac{3}{4}$ cup water and diced tomatoes. Turn heat to low and simmer for 7 to 10 minutes.

c) Top with shredded cheese and green onions. Do not stir.

d) When cheese is melted, serve over a bed of lettuce, rice or in flour or corn tortillas!

42. <u>Skirt Steak Street Tacos</u>

Makes: 6 tacos

INGREDIENTS:
- 1 Skirt Steak, cut into 4 to 6-inch portions, in thin strips
- 12 six-inch corn tortillas
- $\frac{1}{2}$ teaspoon salt
- $\frac{1}{4}$ teaspoon cayenne pepper
- $\frac{1}{2}$ teaspoon garlic powder
- $\frac{1}{2}$ teaspoon minced garlic
- 1 teaspoon oil
- 1 cup diced onion
- $\frac{1}{2}$ cup cilantro leaves, roughly chopped
- 2 cups thinly sliced red cabbage
- Cilantro Lime Vinaigrette:
- $\frac{3}{4}$ cup cilantro leaves
- Juice from 2 limes
- $\frac{1}{3}$ cup olive oil
- 4 teaspoons minced garlic
- $\frac{1}{4}$ cup white vinegar
- 4 teaspoons sugar
- $\frac{1}{4}$ cup milk
- $\frac{1}{2}$ cup sour cream

INSTRUCTIONS:
a) Heat oil over medium heat. Season sliced steak with salt, cayenne pepper and garlic powder. Add steak to pan and sauté until cooked through (8 to 10 minutes). Add garlic and sauté 1 to 2 minutes longer until garlic is fragrant. Remove from heat and dice steak.

b) Whisk together all ingredients for vinaigrette. Add mixture to a blender and pulse until smooth, about 1 to 2 minutes.

c) Fill warmed corn tortillas (use two per taco) with steak, onion, chopped cilantro and cabbage. Drizzle with vinaigrette and serve.

43. Puerto Rican Taco

INGREDIENTS:

- Corn taco shells
- Cheese
- Cooked ground beef
- A Sweet yellow plantains (cooked and cut into chunks)

INSTRUCTIONS:

a) Place two big spoons of ground beef in your tortilla.
b) Add two plantain pieces to your tortilla.
c) Put a little cheese on top, and it's ready to eat!
d) Enjoy!

44. Meaty Taco Casserole

INGREDIENTS:
- 1 lb ground beef
- 1 onion, chopped
- 1 (10-ounce) can enchilada sauce or salsa
- 1 (8-ounce) can tomato sauce
- 1 (15-ounce) can black beans, rinsed and drained
- 1 cup frozen corn
- 1 (8-10 count) can reduced-fat refrigerator biscuits
- 1 cup shredded reduced-fat Mexican blend cheese
- ⅓ cup chopped green onions

INSTRUCTIONS:
a) Preheat oven to 350°F.

b) Coat 13 x 9 x 2-inch baking dish with nonstick cooking spray.

c) In a large nonstick skillet, cook the meat and onion until the meat is done; drain excess fat.

d) Mix the enchilada sauce or salsa, tomato sauce, and black beans and corn, stirring well. Tear biscuits into fourths.

e) Stir the veggie mixture into the meat mixture, then transfer it to the baking dish. Mix in the biscuit chunks last.

f) Bake 25 minutes. Remove it from the oven, and sprinkle it with cheese and green onions. Return the baking dish to the oven and bake 5-7 minutes more, or until the cheese is melted.

45. Beef Cilantro Taco

INGREDIENTS:

- 1 package soft corn or wheat tortillas
- 2 tablespoons chili powder
- 1 tablespoon ground cumin
- $\frac{1}{2}$ teaspoon cayenne pepper
- 2 teaspoons kosher salt
- 2 tablespoons vegetable oil
- 1 large white onion, chopped
- 16 ounces ground beef
- 2 cloves garlic, minced
- $\frac{2}{3}$ cup beef broth
- Mexican Blend Shredded Cheese, to taste
- All Natural Sour Cream, to taste
- 1 large tomato, seeds removed, chopped
- $\frac{1}{4}$ cup fresh cilantro leaves, chopped

INSTRUCTIONS:

a) Combine chili powder, cumin, cayenne pepper and salt in a small jar and shake to combine. Set aside. Heat oil in a large cast-iron skillet on medium-high heat.

b) When oil shimmers, sauté half of the chopped onion until translucent and starting to brown, about 3 to 4 minutes.

c) Add ground beef and garlic and cook until browned, about 3 to 4 minutes. Add jar of combined spices and beef broth. Stir to combine.

d) Bring to a simmer and cook until thick, about 2 to 3 minutes.

e) Once the sauce thickens, turn heat down.

f) Combine the reserved chopped onion, chopped tomato and chopped cilantro. Place in small bowl.

g) Assemble tacos by placing a small amount of cheese in the center of a tortilla, then add some hot meat/sauce mixture to melt the cheese.

h) Top with onion-tomato-cilantro mixture and a dollop of sour cream. Roll up and enjoy!

46. Tomato Soup beef tacos

Makes: 24 Servings

INGREDIENTS:
- 2 pounds Ground beef
- $\frac{1}{2}$ cup Chopped green pepper
- 1 can Beef broth
- 1 can Tomato soup
- 2 tablespoons Chopped cherry peppers
- 24 Taco shells
- 1 Shredded cheddar cheese
- 1 Shredded Monterey jack
- 1 Chopped onion
- 1 Shredded lettuce
- 1 Diced tomatoes

INSTRUCTIONS:
a) In frying pan, brown beef and cook green pepper until tender; stir to separate meat.

b) Add soups and cherry peppers. Cook over low heat 5 minutes; stir occasionally.

c) Fill each taco shell with 3-4 Tablespoons meat mixture; top each with remaining ingredients.

47. Grilled lamb with soft tacos

Makes: 1 serving

INGREDIENTS:
- 1 pounds Trimmed boneless leg of lamb; or sirloin steaks
- 3 Cloves garlic; mashed
- 1½ Inch piece fresh ginger; peeled and minced
- ½ cup Mild jalapeno jelly or jam
- 4 Flour tortillas
- Salsa for garnish

INSTRUCTIONS:
a) Cut lamb into ½-inch slices; set aside. Combine the garlic, ginger, and jelly.
b) Spread the ginger mixture on each slice of lamb.
c) Meanwhile, preheat an outdoor grill, stovetop grill, or heavy, seasoned skillet to medium-high.
d) To cook, separate the lamb slices and place them on the grill or in the skillet; sear for two to three minutes per side, until medium rare.
e) Meanwhile, warm the tortillas in a plastic bag in the microwave for one minute, or briefly over a burner.
f) Divide the filling among the tortillas, and wrap each tortilla around the filling. Serve with a bowl of salsa, if desired.

48. <u>Grilled pork tacos & papaya salsa</u>

Makes: 5 Servings

INGREDIENTS:
- 1 Papaya; peeled, seeded, cut in $\frac{1}{2}$ inch cubes
- 1 small Red chili; seeded and fine chopped
- $\frac{1}{2}$ cup Red onion; chopped
- $\frac{1}{2}$ cup Red bell pepper; chopped
- $\frac{1}{2}$ cup Fresh mint leaves; chopped
- 2 tablespoons Lime juice
- $\frac{1}{4}$ pounds Pork boneless center loin roast; cut into strips
- $\frac{1}{2}$ cup Fresh papaya; chopped
- $\frac{1}{2}$ cup Fresh pineapple; chopped
- 10 Flour tortillas, warmed
- $1\frac{1}{2}$ cup Monterey Jack cheese; shredded (6 oz)
- 2 tablespoons Margarine or butter; melted

INSTRUCTIONS:
a) Cook pork in 10-inch skillet over medium heat about 10 minutes, stirring occasionally, until no longer pink; drain.

b) Stir in papaya and pineapple. Heat, stirring occasionally, until hot. Heat oven to 425F.

c) Spoon about $\frac{1}{4}$ cup of the pork mixture onto half of each tortilla; top with about 2 tablespoons of the cheese.

d) Fold tortillas over filling. Arrange five of the filled tortillas in ungreased jelly roll pan, 15 $\frac{1}{2}$x10 $\frac{1}{2}$x1 inch; brush with melted margarine.

e) Bake uncovered about 10 minutes or until light golden brown. Repeat with remaining tacos. Serve with Papaya Salsa.

49. Shredded Pork Tacos

Makes: 12 servings

INGREDIENTS:
- ½ pound pork roast

- 12 soft homemade tacos
- 1 cup sliced onions
- $\frac{1}{2}$ cup chopped tomatoes & 1 avocado
- 1 can tomatoes & 2-3 jalapeno chiles
- $\frac{1}{2}$ cup sour cream sauce
- 1 ancho chili & 1 cup water
- 1 cup shredded lettuce
- $\frac{1}{2}$ teaspoon salt & pepper
- 1 cup shredded cheddar cheese

INSTRUCTIONS:

a) Take a large saucepan and add the chopped pork meat, vegetables, water and seasonings, cooking for 20 minutes stirring occasionally. Remove the vegetables and chicken meat from the cooking liquid and shred them into small pieces.

b) Assemble the homemade tortillas with lettuce, pork meat, vegetables, sour cream sauce, shredded cheese, diced tomatoes, and avocados.

50. Pork and Eggs Taco

Makes: 5-6

INGREDIENTS:
- 10 tortillas
- Fully cooked pork sausages (1 packet)
- 3 eggs
- $\frac{1}{2}$ cup cheddar cheese, roughly shredded
- 1 avocado, sliced
- Salt
- Pepper

INSTRUCTIONS:
a) Whip up the eggs with salt and pepper and cook them over high flame.

b) Make sure you cook both sides for approximately one minute each.

c) Heat the sausages according to the instructions on your packet menu.

d) You could also substitute the sausages for any other protein food you have at home including leftover meat, chicken or vegetables.

e) Remove the eggs and warm the tortillas. Turn off the heat and simply use the heat from the still-hot girdle to do so.

f) Slice the egg according to the number of tortillas and place a piece of egg, sausage, avocado, cheese and garnishing of your preference. You can also add bacon and hash browns.

g) Serve with lime and salsa.

51. Pork Carnitas Tacos

Makes: 8

INGREDIENTS:
- 1½ kg pork shoulder cut, chopped into 1 ½-inch pieces
- ½ kg pork belly, sliced into small pieces
- 1 cup chicken stock
- 1 tablespoon salt
- 1 teaspoon black pepper
- 8 corn tortillas

INSTRUCTIONS:
a) Boil the pork shoulder, pork belly, salt and pepper in a large pot. Simmer

b) for at least two hours or until the pork is tender enough to shred easily.

c) Reduce the liquid for ten minutes before removing the pot.

d) Place half the boiled pork (and the juices) in a large skillet and cook it on high heat until the pork begins to sizzle in its own fat. Once the pork begins to turn brown and crisp, remove from the skillet. Repeat the process with the rest of the pork.

e) Place the pork in a tortilla, garnish with veggies of your choice such as sliced avocados, shredded cabbage, onions, zucchini, bell peppers, lime and sauce.

52. Taco Truck Tacos

Makes: 4 servings

INGREDIENTS:
- 1½ pounds pork shoulder (shredded)

- 2 Limes
- 12 corn tortillas
- 1 bunch cilantro
- ½ cup chopped onions
- Radishes, avocado & fresh Tomatoes

INSTRUCTIONS:

a) Into a medium pan start browning the meat which was previously seasoned with cumin, salt, and pepper.

b) When done, warm the tortillas over both sides and top them with the meat, onions, avocado, tomatoes and some lime juice.

53. <u>Tacos with Grilled Kielbasa</u>

Makes: 4

INGREDIENTS:
- 1 red onion (cut into 4 pieces)
- 2 bell peppers (red, and cut lengthwise. Remove seeds)
- 1 bunch of scallions
- 3 tablespoons olive oil
- Salt
- Pepper
- ⅓ cup lime juice
- 750 grams kielbasa sausage, halve vertically
- 8 corn tortillas
- cilantro

INSTRUCTIONS:
a) Toss the onion, bell peppers, and scallions together with oil over a grill that has been set to medium high heat.
b) Season with salt and pepper and grill until the vegetables get a slightly charred look.
c) Remember to take the scallions off after 2 minutes though!
d) Take them off the heat and let it cool.
e) Slice the onion into wedges that are 1-inch long and toss with lime juice. Similarly, remove the skin off the bell peppers, cut them into wedges that are 1-inch long and place in a separate bowl. The scallions should be placed on a different platter.
f) Grill the sausages for about 5 minutes each and place them with the scallions.
g) Grill the tortillas to give a slightly charred look.

h)Pile all the ingredients into each tortilla and serve with hot sauce and fresh lime for squeezing over.

54. Picadillo tacos

Makes: 1 serving

INGREDIENTS:

- $\frac{1}{2}$ cup Raisins
- $\frac{1}{4}$ cup Tequila
- $\frac{1}{2}$ pounds Bulk pork sausage
- $\frac{1}{2}$ pounds Ground beef
- 1 medium Onion, chopped
- 3 Cloves garlic, minced
- 1 can (14 $\frac{1}{2}$ oz) whole tomatoes, cut up, UNDRAINED
- 1 can (4 oz) diced green chili peppers, drained
- 2 tablespoons Sugar
- 1 teaspoon Ground cinnamon
- $\frac{1}{4}$ teaspoon Ground cumin
- 1 dash Ground cloves
- 12 7 inch flour tortillas
- ⅓ cup Pecans, finely chopped
- Shredded lettuce, optional

INSTRUCTIONS:

a) In a small saucepan, combine raisins and tequila. Bring to boiling; remove from heat. Let stand for 5 minutes.

b) For filling: In a large skillet cook sausage, beef, onion, and garlic over medium heat till meat is brown. Drain off fat. Stir in undrained raisins, undrained tomatoes, green chili peppers, sugar, cinnamon, cumin and cloves.

c) Bring to boiling; reduce heat. Simmer, uncovered for about 30 minutes or until most of the liquid is evaporated.

d) Meanwhile, wrap tortillas in foil. Heat in a 350 oven for 10 minutes or until warm. Stir pecans into meat mixture.

e) To serve, top warm tortillas with lettuce, then filling. Fold or roll up.

55. <u>Pork tacos, California style</u>

Makes: 6 servings

INGREDIENTS:

- 2 pounds Pork tenderloin
- 6 Green onions
- 12 smalls Fresh corn tortillas
- 1 bunch Cilantro; large stems removed
- Guacamole
- 1 cup Sour cream
- 1 cup Spicy Red Salsa
- 1 cup Green Chile Salsa

FOR THE MARINADE

- $\frac{1}{2}$ cup Freshly-squeezed orange juice
- 2 tablespoons Freshly-squeezed lime juice
- 1 teaspoon Chopped fresh oregano
- $\frac{1}{4}$ teaspoon Cumin
- $\frac{1}{2}$ teaspoon Marjoram
- $\frac{1}{2}$ teaspoon Salt
- $\frac{1}{4}$ teaspoon Finely-ground black pepper

INSTRUCTIONS:

a) Combine marinade ingredients in a medium bowl.

b) Whisk until blended. Place pork in a shallow non-aluminum dish and pour marinade over it. Marinate for 6 to 12 hours, refrigerated.

c) Cut through green part of onion, making 2 slits all the way down to where the white part begins. This will give the onions a fan shape.

d) Preheat oven to 350 degrees. Preheat grill pan over moderately-high heat. Grill pork for 15 to 20 minutes on each side, or until interior temperature is 160 degrees.

e) Baste green onions with marinade and grill for about 3 minutes on each side. Remove meat and onions from grill, cut meat into small chunks, and reserve.

f) Wrap tortillas in aluminum foil and warm in oven for about 10 minutes.

g) Keep warm while preparing plates. On outer edges of individual serving plates, arrange a few sprigs of cilantro, a large dollop of Guacamole, and a large dollop of sour cream.

h) Place 2 warmed tortillas on side of each plate and arrange meat and grilled scallions in center.

i) Pass Spicy Red and Green Chile Salsas in separate bowls.

j) Serve immediately.

56. Honey-Cilantro Shrimp Soft Tacos

Makes: 4 servings

INGREDIENTS:
- 8 tortillas

- 1 teaspoon vegetable oil
- $\frac{1}{2}$ tablespoons salt and pepper
- 1 large onion & 1 jalapeno
- 3 bell peppers
- 2 teaspoon coriander & cumin
- 2-4 garlic cloves
- 4 tablespoons fresh cilantro & honey
- 1 $\frac{1}{2}$ pounds cocktail shrimp

INSTRUCTIONS:

a) Cook the shrimps, jalapeno, onion, bell peppers, seasonings and garlic into a medium skillet until they get tender.

b) Into a glass bowl, combine the fresh cilantro and honey, until a smooth mixture is formed.

c) Spoon the mixture over each tortilla; add the shrimps and some salsa sauce.

57. Baja Fish Tacos

Makes: 4 servings

INGREDIENTS:
- 1 ½ pounds thawed fresh tilapia filets

- 4 medium whole wheat tortillas
- 1 tablespoon fresh cilantro
- 1 onion, avocado and tomato (all chopped)
- 2 teaspoon taco seasonings
- 2 cups cabbage slaw
- 1 lemon (juice)

INSTRUCTIONS:
a) Finely chop the vegetables and shred the cabbage into small pieces.
b) After seasoning the tilapia filets with taco seasoning, cook them into an oiled nonstick pan for 5-6 minutes.
c) Slowly cook the fish on both sides and add some onions, lemon juice, and tomatoes over.
d) Warm each tortilla for 1 minute in the microwave, then add the fish filets, vegetables, cabbage, cilantro, and salsa.

58. Shrimp Tacos

Makes: 5 servings

INGREDIENTS:
- 1 pound peeled shrimp

- 10 corn tortillas
- $\frac{1}{2}$ cup sour cream
- 1 tablespoon seasonings & 1 chipotle pepper
- 2 limes (for juice)
- $\frac{1}{2}$ cup chopped purple cabbage
- 2 tablespoons virgin olive oil

INSTRUCTIONS:

a) Combine the chipotle, half the lime juice and sour cream into a small bowl until a smooth paste gets formed.

b) Into a preheated skillet start, cook the peeled shrimps with some seasonings.

c) Warm up each taco and serve them topped with shredded cabbage, chipotle cream, fried shrimps, and sauce.

59. Fish Tacos with Cilantro Slaw and Chipotle Mayo

Makes: 4 servings

INGREDIENTS:
- 1 pound tilapia fish fillets
- 4 flour tortillas
- $\frac{1}{2}$ cup fresh lime juice
- 2 cups 3-color coleslaw blend
- $\frac{1}{4}$ cup mayonnaise
- 1 chipotle chilies soaked in adobo sauce
- 1 cup minced fresh cilantro leaves
- 1 avocado & 1 diced tomato
- 1 tablespoon adobo sauce from chipotle peppers
- $\frac{1}{4}$ teaspoon salt & cayenne pepper
- salt and ground black pepper

INSTRUCTIONS:
a) Pour the lime juice over each tilapia fish filets and keep them into the refrigerator for 4 hours.

b) Start preparing the chipotle mayonnaise dressing by mixing the adobo sauce, cayenne pepper, chilies, $\frac{1}{4}$ teaspoon salt and mayonnaise into a medium bowl, mixing everything.

c) Take the fish out from the fridge and sauté it for 2-3 minutes into an oiled medium pan.

d) Spread 1 tablespoon of chipotle sauce over each tortilla, add the cooked fish, veggies, and seasonings.

60. Grilled Shrimp and Black Bean Tacos

Makes: 6 servings

INGREDIENTS:
- 1 pound Peeled shrimp

- 12 corn tortillas
- 2 tablespoons chili powder
- 1 $\frac{1}{2}$ tablespoons squeezed lime juice
- 1 cup black beans
- Pico de Gallo
- $\frac{1}{2}$ teaspoon virgin olive oil
- $\frac{1}{4}$ teaspoon salt
- 6 Skewers

INSTRUCTIONS:

a) Preheat your grill, then prepare the sauce, heating up the black beans, lime juice, chili powder and salt into a medium pan.

b) When a smooth paste is formed, prepare the shrimp skewers. They need to be fried for about 1-2 minutes for both sides, then brush each shrimp and grill them for another 2 minutes.

c) Build your tortilla, adding the shrimps, sauce and seasonings.

61. <u>Blackened Cabo Fish Tacos</u>

Makes: 4 servings

INGREDIENTS:
- 1½ pounds white fish & 8 ounces fish marinade

- 12 corn tortillas
- ¾ pound Asian Slaw
- 9 tablespoons lime sour cream
- 4 ounces butter
- 7 tablespoons chipotle aioli
- 7 tablespoons Pico de Gallo
- 2 tablespoons black pepper spice
- Chipotle Aioli
- ¾ cup mayonnaise
- 1 teaspoon lime juice
- 1 tablespoon mustard
- Kosher salt & ground black pepper
- 2 chipotle peppers

INSTRUCTIONS:

a) Into a medium saucepan, start melting the unsalted butter, add the marinated white fish, sprinkle some black pepper spice and fry them for 2 minutes on both sides.

b) Warm each tortilla over both sides, add the fried chicken, the chipotle aioli sauce, a few Pico de Gallo, some Asian slaw and some seasonings.

62. Spicy Shrimp Tacos

Makes: 2 servings

INGREDIENTS:
- 4 low-carb tortillas

- 4 tablespoons mango salsa sauce
- 16 large shrimps
- 1 tablespoon fresh chopped cilantro
- 1 cup Romaine lettuce
- $\frac{1}{2}$ cup cheddar cheese
- 4 teaspoon chili sauce
- $\frac{1}{2}$ cup sauteed onions
- Juice of 1 lime

INSTRUCTIONS:

a) Start with the shrimps by marinating and skewering them into the siracha sauce for 5 minutes.

b) Turn on the grill and cook the onions for a few minutes, until well cooked.

c) Lay down each tortilla and top with sour cream, shrimps, lettuce, shredded cheese, grilled onions and other seasonings.

63. Tilapia Tacos

Makes: 1 serving

INGREDIENTS:
- 1 pound Tilapia fish filet
- 2 white corn tortillas
- $\frac{1}{2}$ sliced avocado
- $\frac{1}{4}$ teaspoon olive oil
- 1 tomato
- 1 white onion
- 1 lime juice
- 1 handful of cilantro

INSTRUCTIONS:
a) Into a heated oven start broiling the tortillas and tilapia fish filet on both sides, but season the fish with some olive oil, salt and pepper. Into a medium bowl, mix the tomato, lime juice, onion and the seasonings.

b) Place a nice layer of shredded fish over each tortilla, add the mixture from the bowl, sliced avocado, then place the remaining fish on the top.

64. <u>Mojito-Grilled Fish Tacos with Lime Slaw Topping</u>

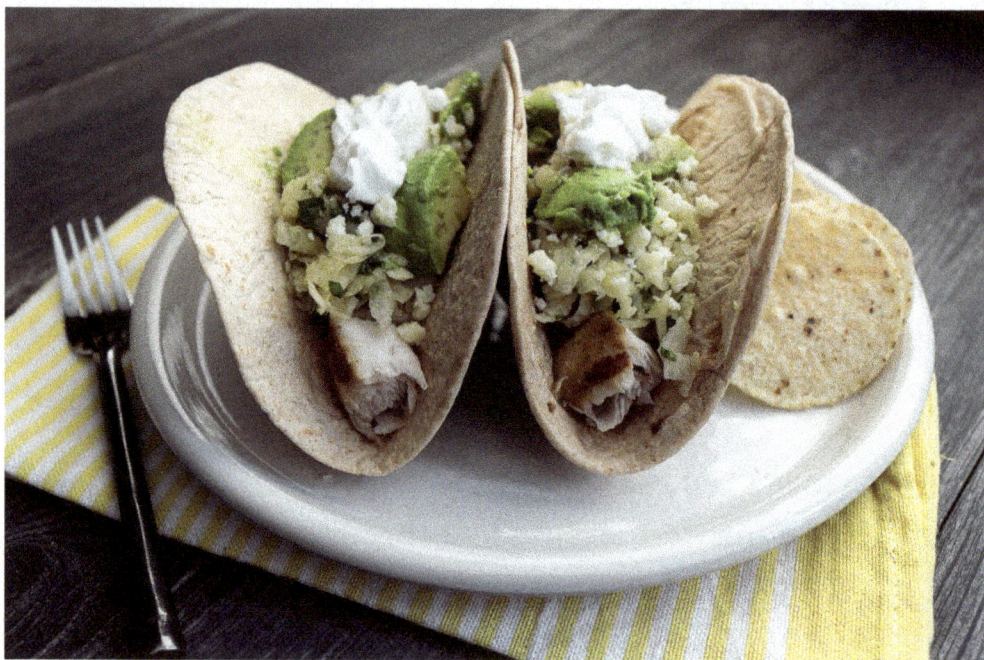

Makes: 8 servings

INGREDIENTS:
- 8 corn tortillas

- 2 tablespoons lime juice
- 2 tablespoons minced mint leaves
- 1 pound firm white fish (halibut, snapper or cod)
- 1 tablespoon canola oil
- 1 fresh jalapeno chile
- $\frac{1}{2}$ teaspoon salt & 1 teaspoon sugar
- Lime Slaw
- 2 tablespoons minutest
- $\frac{1}{2}$ cup low-fat mayonnaise
- 1 $\frac{1}{2}$ cups shredded cabbage
- 1 tablespoon fresh lime juice

INSTRUCTIONS:

a) Start combining the fish and marinade ingredients together, then place it into the fridge for 3 minutes. When done, take the fish out and start grill it over both sides, until it gets nice and firm.

b) For preparing the lime slaw, add the cabbage, mayonnaise, lime juice and mint into a medium bowl, stirring everything well.

c) Place the fish on each tortilla, add some slaw spoons and vegetables.

65. Grilled fish tacos with cilantro sauce

Makes: 2 servings

INGREDIENTS:
SAUCE
- $\frac{1}{4}$ cup green onions & cilantro
- 2 $\frac{1}{2}$ tablespoons mayonnaise
- 3 tablespoons sour cream
- 2 limes (juice)
- $\frac{1}{2}$ teaspoon salt, pepper & 1 garlic clove

FISH
- 2 pounds red snapper steaks
- 4 corn tortillas
- 2 $\frac{1}{2}$ cans cabbage
- 1 tablespoon ground cumin & coriander
- $\frac{1}{2}$ teaspoon red pepper, paprika & garlic salt

INSTRUCTIONS:
a) Start combining the cilantro sauce ingredients in a medium bowl, then set it aside.

b) For the fish, season it with some garlic powder, cumin, paprika, coriander and red pepper, grilling it for 5 minutes on both sides.

c) Once the fish is done, cut it lengthwise and place it on tortillas, add the cabbage and 1 tablespoon of cilantro sauce on top.

66. Healthy Fish Tacos

INGREDIENTS:

- 1 pound white flaky fish, such as mahi mahi
- $\frac{1}{4}$ cup canola oil
- 1 lime, juiced
- 1 tablespoon ancho chili powder
- 1 jalapeno, coarsely chopped
- $\frac{1}{4}$ cup chopped fresh cilantro leaves
- 8 flour tortillas
- Shredded white cabbage
- Hot sauce
- Crema or sour cream
- Thinly sliced red onion
- Thinly sliced green onion
- Chopped cilantro leaves

INSTRUCTIONS:

a) Preheat grill to medium-high. Place the fish in a dish and add oil, lime juice, jalapeno, ancho, and cilantro. Mix well to coat the fish and let it marinate for 20 minutes.

b) Remove fish from marinade and grill it flesh side down. Grill for 4 minutes then flip and grill for 30 seconds to a minute.

c) Let it rest for 5 minutes before flaking with a fork.

d) Grill the tortillas for 20 seconds.

e) Distribute the fish into each tacos and garnish with cabbage, onions, cilantro.

f) Drizzle with hot sauce and add your choice of salsa.

67. Cajun shrimp tacos with tomatillo salsa

Makes: 8 Servings

INGREDIENTS:
- 2 cups Sour cream
- 2 teaspoons Chili powder
- $\frac{1}{2}$ teaspoon Cayenne pepper
- $\frac{3}{4}$ pounds Tomatillos, husks removed, rinsed, quartered
- $\frac{1}{2}$ cup Coarsely chopped unpeeled green apple
- 2 tablespoons Coarsely chopped fresh basil
- 2 tablespoons Coarsely chopped fresh mint
- $1\frac{1}{2}$ teaspoon Chili powder
- $1\frac{1}{2}$ teaspoon Paprika
- 2 pounds Uncooked medium shrimp, peeled, deveined
- 2 tablespoons Olive oil
- 1 tablespoon Minced garlic
- 16 Purchased taco shells
- 1 large Bunch watercress, trimmed
- 2 Avocados, peeled, pitted, cubed

INSTRUCTIONS:
FOR SOUR CREAM:
a) Whisk all ingredients in medium bowl to blend. Season with salt.
FOR SALSA:
b) Finely chop tomatillos, apple, basil and mint in food processor.
c) Transfer to small bowl. Season to taste with salt.
FOR SHRIMP:
d) Combine chili powder and paprika in large bowl. Add shrimp; toss to coat.

e) Let stand 5 minutes. Heat oil in heavy large skillet over high heat.

f) Add garlic and sauté until fragrant, about 1 minute. Add shrimp; sauté until opaque in center, about 5 minutes.

g) Season with salt and pepper. Transfer to a small bowl.

h) Preheat oven to 350°F. Arrange taco shells on heavy large baking sheet. Bake until hot, about 8 minutes. Place shells in napkin-lined basket.

i) Arrange half of watercress on platter.

j) Top with shrimp. Chop remaining watercress. Place in small bowl.

k) Place sour cream, salsa, avocados and chopped watercress in separate bowls.

68. Ceviche tacos

Makes: 4 Servings

INGREDIENTS:
- 1½ pounds Red snapper fillets; in ½ inch chunks
- Juice of 10 limes
- 1 Onion; finely chopped
- 1 Jalapeno pepper; seeded/finely chopped
- 14½ ounce Can tomatoes
- ½ cup Corn kernels
- ¼ cup Chopped cilantro
- 2 tablespoons Olive oil
- 2 tablespoons Catsup
- 1 tablespoon Worcestershire sauce
- ½ teaspoon Dried oregano
- Salt; to taste
- 8 Corn tortillas
- 1 Red onion; thinly sliced
- 1 Avocado; peeled/sliced

INSTRUCTIONS:
a) In a large glass or non-reactive aluminum bowl, gently combine fish and lime juice. Cover, refrigerate, and marinate overnight.

b) When you remove fish in morning, it will be "cooked" through and safe to eat.

c) When ready to serve the tacos, combine onion, jalapeno, tomatoes, corn cilantro, olive oil, catsup, Worcestershire sauce and oregano in a large glass bowl. Mix well. Season with salt to taste.

d) Drain and rinse fish, add to tomato mixture and gently mix to coat.

e) Heat tortillas in microwave or oven. Place $\frac{1}{8}$ of fish mixture in tortilla and garnish with red onion and avocado.

69. Grilled fish tacos with green salsa

Makes: 4 Servings

INGREDIENTS:
- $3\frac{1}{2}$ cup Finely shredded red or green cabbage
- $\frac{1}{4}$ cup White distilled vinegar
- Salt and pepper
- $\frac{3}{4}$ pounds Fresh tomatillos
- 2 tablespoons Salad oil
- 1 Onion, cut into $\frac{1}{2}$ inch slices
- $1\frac{1}{2}$ pounds Firm-fleshed skinned fish fillets (lingcod, sea bass)
- 4 Jalapeno chilies
- 2 teaspoons Lime juice
- $\frac{3}{4}$ cup Fresh cilantro leaves
- 1 Clove garlic
- 12 Warm corn or low-fat flour tortillas (6-7 inch)
- Low-fat sour cream
- Lime wedges

INSTRUCTIONS:
a) Look for the small green tomatillos with papery husks in some supermarkets and Latino grocery stores.

b) Mix cabbage with vinegar and 3 tablespoons water. Add salt and pepper to taste. Cover and chill.

c) Remove and discard husks from tomatillos; rinse tomatillos.

d) Thread onto skewers. Brush some of the oil lightly onto onion slices. Rinse fish and pat dry. Brush fish with remaining oil.

e) Place tomatillos, onion, and chilies on a barbecue grill.

f) Cook, turning as needed, until vegetables are browned, 8-10 minutes.

g) Set aside to cool.

h) Place fish on grill (med-high heat). Cook, turning once, until fish is opaque but still moist-looking in thickest part (cut to test), 10-14 minutes.

i) Remove stems from chilies; remove seeds.

j) In a blender or food processor, whirl tomatillos, chilies, lime juice, $\frac{1}{4}$ c cilantro, and garlic until smooth. Chop onion. Add the chopped onion to salsa mixture, and salt and pepper to taste.

k) Pour into small bowl.

l) To assemble each taco, fill a tortilla with a little cabbage relish, a few chunks of fish, salsa, and sour cream. Add a squeeze of lime, and salt and pepper to taste.

70. Margarita shrimp tacos

Makes: 6 Servings

INGREDIENTS:
- 1½ pounds Shell-on Shrimp; uncooked
- ½ cup Tequila
- ½ cup Lime juice
- 1 teaspoon Salt
- 1 Clove minced Garlic clove; or more to taste
- 3 tablespoons Olive oil; or less
- 2 tablespoons Chopped cilantro
- 24 Flour tortillas; (6 or 7 inches)
- Shredded lettuce
- 1 Avocado; sliced; or more
- Salsa fresca; as needed
- 1 can (15 oz) Black beans
- 1 can (10 oz) Corn kernels
- ½ cup Chopped red onion
- ¼ cup Olive oil
- 2 tablespoons Lime juice
- ¼ teaspoon Ground cumin
- ¼ teaspoon Oregano
- ¼ teaspoon Salt

INSTRUCTIONS:
a) Peel and devein shrimp, retaining tails, if desired; set aside. Combine tequila, lime juice, salt; pour over shrimp and marinate no more than 1 hour.
b) Sauté minced garlic in 1 tablespoon oil until light brown; add shrimp, cook and stir until done, 2 to 3 minutes. Add oil as needed.

c) Sprinkle with cilantro and keep warm. For each taco, fold 2 soft tortillas together; fill with shredded lettuce and Black Bean and Corn Relish.

d) Top with shrimp, avocado slices and salsa.

e) Black Bean and Corn Relish: Rinse and drain beans; drain corn,

f) Combine beans and corn with remaining ingredients; refrigerate to blend flavors.

71. <u>Salmon tacos</u>

Makes: 8 Tacos

INGREDIENTS:
- 418 grams Canned Alaska salmon
- 8 tablespoons Fromage frais
- 50 grams Cucumber; sliced
- ½ teaspoon Mint
- 8 Ready-made taco shells
- 100 grams Iceberg lettuce, shredded
- 3 Tomatoes; chopped
- 50 grams Cheddar cheese, grated
- Olives, anchovies, or chopped peppers to garnish

INSTRUCTIONS:
a) Pre-heat the oven to 200 C, 400 F, Gas mark 6.

b) Drain the can of salmon. Flake the fish and set aside. Mix together the fromage frais or Greek yogurt, cucumber and mint. Set aside.

c) Heat the taco shells in the oven for 2-3 minutes until pliable.

d) Pile lettuce and tomato into each shell then top with chunks of salmon, a spoonful of the cucumber mixture and some grated cheese.

e) Garnish and serve immediately.

72. <u>Seafood tacos with corn salsa</u>

Makes: 4 Servings

INGREDIENTS:
- 1 pounds Rockfish fillets
- 2 Limes; juice of
- 2 teaspoons Olive oil
- 8 Fresh corn tortillas
- 1 cup Corn kernels; cooked
- 1 medium Red onion; chopped
- 1 cup Seeded chopped cucumber
- 2 Jalapeno peppers; minced, or to taste
- $\frac{1}{2}$ bunch Cilantro; chopped
- $\frac{1}{2}$ cup Chopped red bell pepper
- $\frac{1}{2}$ teaspoon Salt; to taste
- $\frac{1}{2}$ teaspoon Pepper; to taste
- 2 Limes; juice of
- Lettuce leaves or shredded cabbage; optional
- Lime wedges; optional
- Cilantro sprigs; optional

INSTRUCTIONS:
a) Marinate fish in lime juice and olive oil for 30 minutes.
b) Grill fish on barbecue or broil in oven for 10 minutes total per inch of thickness, about 5 minutes per side. Fish is ready when flesh turns opaque in center.
c) Heat tortillas until pliable. With 2 tortillas halfway overlapping each other, place fish in center and garnish to taste. Use toothpicks or roll in waxed paper to hold tacos together.
CORN SALSA

d) In medium bowl, combine all ingredients. Let set 1 hour to blend flavors.

73. Soft tacos with red snapper

Makes: 4 Servings

INGREDIENTS:
- $\frac{1}{4}$ cup Olive oil
- 2 Red onions, halved and Sliced thin
- 1 teaspoon Salt
- $1\frac{1}{2}$ teaspoon Pepper
- 2 teaspoons Minced fresh thyme
- $1\frac{1}{2}$ pounds Red snapper, cut into bite- Size pieces
- 1 teaspoon Minced garlic
- 2 teaspoons Lime juice
- 2 teaspoons Soy sauce
- 2 teaspoons Minced fresh oregano
- 8 Soft corn tortillas, warmed
- 3 cups Shredded lettuce

INSTRUCTIONS:
a) In a skillet heat 2 tablespoons oil over moderately high heat until hot. Add onions, salt, $\frac{1}{2}$ teaspoon pepper, and thyme and sauté until rich golden in color.

b) Heat another skillet over moderately high heat until hot and add remaining 2 tablespoons oil. Swirl and add snapper.

c) Sauté for 2 minutes, turning frequently, add garlic, lime juice, and soy sauce and sauté until liquid is nearly evaporated and snapper is lightly golden in color.

d) Add oregano and remaining pepper and toss to combine. Add onion mixture and toss well.

e) Fill tortillas with lettuce and top with snapper and onion mixture.

74. <u>Fresh Fruit Tacos</u>

INGREDIENTS:

- Whole wheat tortillas (small)
- Water
- Ground cinnamon
- Sugar
- Greek yogurt (vanilla flavored)
- Your choice of fresh fruit (diced):
- Strawberries
- Mangos
- Pineapples
- Kiwis

INSTRUCTIONS:

a) Preheat oven to 325°F.

b) Using a round, plastic cookie cutter, cut small circles from the whole wheat tortillas (approx. 2 per small tortilla).

c) Lay these little tortillas on a baking pan. Place water in a small bowl; lightly coat the top side of the tortillas with water, using a basting brush.

d) Mix a small amount of ground cinnamon and sugar in a bowl; dust the moist tortillas with the cinnamon and sugar mixture.

e) Using tongs, individually drape each tortilla over the wire rack in the toaster oven, allowing the sides of the tortilla to fall between two metal bars on the rack.

f) Bake approx. 5-7 minutes, checking the tortillas periodically.

g) Using tongs, lift the tortillas off of the rack and transfer to a cooling rack; tortillas should remain in this upside down position to cool, which is the final step in forming the taco shape.

h) Transfer the cooled taco shells to a plate and place a dollop of vanilla Greek yogurt in the tortilla shell; use a spoon to smooth and cover the bottom and sides of the shell.

i) Spoon your favorite fruit into the shell, and enjoy!

75. Fruit filled low-fat cocoa tacos

Makes: 6 Servings

INGREDIENTS:
- $\frac{1}{4}$ cup Flour
- $\frac{1}{4}$ cup Sugar
- 1 tablespoon Baking cocoa
- 2 tablespoons 2% milk
- 2 tablespoons Oil
- 1 Egg white
- 1 teaspoon Vanilla extract
- Salt to taste
- 8 ounces Fruit flavored low-fat yogurt
- 4 Kiwi fruit; peeled, sliced
- 6 larges Strawberries; sliced
- 8 ounces Mango coulis
- 1 ounce Raspberry sauce
- 1 pint Fresh raspberries
- 6 Sprigs fresh mint

INSTRUCTIONS:
a) Combine first 8 ingredients in bowl; beat until smooth. Chill, covered, for 2 hours.

b) Place 3 tablespoonfuls at a time in heated nonstick 8-inch skillet over medium heat. Cook for 2 minutes or until batter appears dry; turn. Cook for 1 minute longer. Remove and drape over wire rack; cool for 15 to 20 minutes.

c) Spread yogurt over half of each baked shell. Alternate 5 slices kiwi fruit and 5 slices strawberry on yogurt. Fold shells over to form tacos.

d) Spread mango coulis in 3x4-inch ovals on bottom halves of 6 plates.

e) Pipe raspberry sauce in 2 stripes across coulis. Swirl through sauces with knife.

f) Place 1 taco beside coulis on each plate. Garnish each plate with raspberries and mint.

76. Coconut Fruit tacos

Makes: 6 servings

INGREDIENTS:

- ⅓ cup Baked coconut
- 1 cup Strawberries, sliced
- ½ cup Seedless green grapes, halved
- 1 medium Apple, pared, cored and chopped
- 1 small Banana, sliced
- 2 tablespoons Pourable fruit, any flavor
- 6 Taco shells
- ⅓ cup Vanilla yogurt

INSTRUCTIONS:

a) Spread coconut on baking sheet.

b) Toast in 350 F oven for 7 to 12 minutes, stirring often.

c) Meanwhile, in medium bowl, stir together strawberries, grapes, apple, banana, and pourable fruit.

d) Fill taco shells evenly with fruit.

e) Top filled tacos evenly with yogurt.

f) Sprinkle with toasted coconut.

77. Fried pineapple & orange tacos with grated chocolate

Makes: 6 Servings

INGREDIENTS:
- $\frac{1}{2}$ medium Pineapple; peeled, cored, cut into 1
- 2 Oranges; peeled, seeded, sliced in
- 2 tablespoons Dark brown sugar
- 4 tablespoons Butter
- $1\frac{1}{2}$ tablespoon Confectioners' sugar
- 6 Corn or flour tortillas
- $1\frac{1}{2}$ cup Heavy (whipping) cream
- $\frac{1}{2}$ cup Shredded fresh mint leaves
- 2 ounces Bittersweet chocolate; finely grated

INSTRUCTIONS:
a) Place the pineapple and orange pieces in a large, non-reactive frying pan. Sprinkle with the brown sugar.

b) Cook over medium-high heat until they begin to brown, about 3 minutes.

c) Turn and cook on the other side until the liquid evaporates and the pieces are browned, 2 to 3 minutes more.

d) Remove and set aside.

e) Place 1 tablespoon of the butter and $\frac{1}{2}$ tablespoon of the confectioners' sugar in a frying pan large enough to hold a tortilla.

f) Set over medium-high heat until the butter and sugar melt. Stir.

g) Add a tortilla and fry for 30 seconds.

h) Turn and fry on the other side until browned and slightly crispy, 30 to 45 seconds more. Remove.

i) Continue with the remaining tortillas, adding more butter and sugar to the pan as needed.

j) To assemble, beat the cream until soft peaks form. Spread about ⅓ cup of the pineapple-orange mixture in the center of a sugar-coated tortilla.

k) Top with whipped cream, mint leaves, and a sprinkling of grated chocolate. Fold and serve.

78. Kid's fish taco's

Makes: 1 serving

INGREDIENTS:
- Frozen breaded fish sticks
- Taco sauce
- Lettuce
- Tomato, diced
- Cheddar cheese, grated
- Sour cream
- Taco shells

INSTRUCTIONS:
a) Cook the fish sticks according to package instructions.
b) When cooked, place one fish stick in each taco.
c) Add the various toppings and serve immediately.

79. Ice cream tacos

Makes: 6 Servings

INGREDIENTS:
- 2 tablespoons Sugar
- $\frac{1}{2}$ teaspoon Ground cinnamon
- $1\frac{1}{2}$ tablespoon Butter, melted
- 8 (5 inch) taco shells
- 1 quart Ice cream, any flavor

INSTRUCTIONS:
a) In a cup, combine sugar and cinnamon. Set aside. Lightly brush butter on the inside of each taco shell. sprinkle with sugar mixture, set aside. Remove cover from ice cream carton.

b) Remove ice cream and place on a cutting board.

c) Cut in four slices. Cut each slice in half. Place each half in a prepared taco shell. Arrange ice cream taco's in a 13x9x2 inch baking pan.

d) Cover tightly with plastic wrap or foil and freeze.

e) At serving time, transfer tacos to a platter.

f) Serve with a choice of toppings such as sliced strawberries, blueberries, whipped cream, chopped nuts, toasted coconut, chocolate or caramel sauce.

80. Crunchy Chickpea Tacos

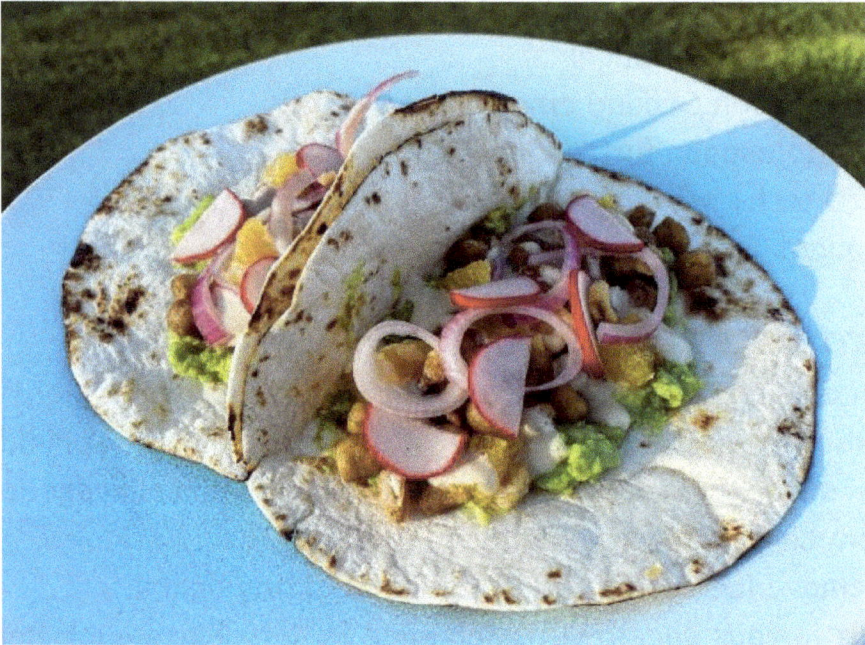

Makes: 6 tacos

INGREDIENTS:
- 6 corn or flour tortillas
- One 15-ounce can chickpeas, rinsed and drained
- $\frac{1}{2}$ teaspoon ancho chili powder
- 3 cups shredded green cabbage
- 1 cup shredded carrot
- $\frac{1}{2}$ cup thinly sliced red onion
- $\frac{1}{2}$ cup seeded and small-diced poblano pepper
- $\frac{1}{2}$ cup sliced green onion
- $\frac{1}{4}$ cup chopped fresh cilantro
- $\frac{1}{4}$ cup Tofu Cashew Mayonnaise 1 serving
- 2 tablespoons lime juice $\frac{1}{4}$ teaspoon sea salt
- 1 avocado, pitted and sliced
- 1 tablespoon Sriracha

INSTRUCTIONS:
a) Preheat the oven to 375°F.

b) Shape the tortillas by placing them in a nonstick oven-safe bowl and baking them in the oven until crispy, 5–10 minutes.

c) In a large mixing bowl, smash the chickpeas with a fork and sprinkle with the chili powder.

d) Add the cabbage, carrot, red onion, poblano pepper, green onion, cilantro, mayonnaise, and lime juice.

e) Mix thoroughly, adding salt last.

f) Divide the salad mixture among the taco bowls and top with the sliced avocado. Add Sriracha if you like your tacos spicy.

81. <u>Tempeh tacos</u>

Makes: 3 to 4 servings

INGREDIENTS:
- Oil, for pan
- 1 package (8 ounces) tempeh
- $1\frac{3}{4}$ cups unsweetened rice milk
- 1 tablespoon Dijon mustard
- 1 tablespoon soy sauce or tamari
- $\frac{1}{2}$ teaspoon paprika
- 2 tablespoons dulse flakes
- 1 tablespoon nutritional yeast
- $\frac{1}{4}$ cup cornmeal
- 13.cup panko-style breadcrumbs
- 1 tablespoon arrowroot Corn tortillas, for tacos
- 1 avocado, sliced

INSTRUCTIONS:
a) Preheat oven to 350 degrees F. Spray a baking sheet with oil. Cut tempeh into 2-inch long and $\frac{1}{2}$-inch thick pieces. Whisk together wet ingredients and set aside.

b) Place dry ingredients in a food processor and pulse a few times, until the mixture is a fine flour. Place in a small bowl. Dredge each piece of tempeh in the rice milk mixture, then toss with breadcrumb mix.

c) Place on baking sheet in three rows about an inch apart. Spray oil on top of pieces, then bake for 15 minutes. Flip and bake another 15 minutes.

d) Serve immediately in corn tortilla with sliced avocado and mango-peach salsa.

82. <u>Mushroom Tacos with Chipotle Cream</u>

Makes: 4

INGREDIENTS:
- 1 medium red onion, thinly sliced
- 1 large portobello mushrooms, diced into ½-inch cubes
- 6 cloves garlic, minced
- Sea salt to taste
- 12 6-inch corn tortillas
- 1 cup Chipotle Cream Sauce
- 2 cups shredded romaine lettuce
- ½ cup chopped fresh cilantro

INSTRUCTIONS:
a) Heat a large skillet over medium-high heat.

b) Add the red onion and portobello mushrooms, and stir-fry for 4 to 5 minutes.

c) Add water 1 to 2 table-spoons at a time to keep the onion and mush-rooms from sticking.

d) Add the garlic and cook for 1 minute. Season with salt.

e) While the mushrooms cook, add 4 tortillas to a nonstick skillet and heat them for a few minutes until they soften.

f) Turn them over and heat for 2 minutes more. Remove

83. Lentil, Kale & Quinoa Tacos

Makes: 8 Servings

INGREDIENTS:
FILLING
- 3 cups quinoa, cooked (1 cup dry)
- 1 cup lentils, cooked ($\frac{1}{2}$ cup dry)
- One batch of Taco Seasoning
- 1 tablespoon coconut oil
- 3 large leaves kale, stems removed, chopped
- Blue-corn taco shells

TOPPINGS
- 2 avocados, pitted, peeled, and sliced
- Fresh cilantro leaves Fresh lime wedges

INSTRUCTIONS:
a) In a large pot heated to medium, fold together cooked quinoa, lentils, Taco Seasoning, coconut oil, and kale. Stir well for 3 – 5 minutes until heat wilts the leaves.

b) Toast taco shells on a parchment-lined baking sheet according to manufacturer's instructions.

c) Load shells with filling, then top with avocado, cilantro, and a squeeze of lime. Serve warm.

84. Corn Salsa Topped Black Bean Tacos

Makes: 4

INGREDIENTS:
- Cooking Olive oil
- 2 cloves Garlic
- 2 ½ cups of black beans, rinsed and drained
- ¼ cup oats
- ¼ cup of cornmeal
- 1 tablespoon red chili powder
- 1 teaspoon kosher salt, divided
- ½ teaspoon black pepper (ground and divided)
- 8 corn tortillas (small)
- 1 cup corn, thawed if frozen
- 1 red bell pepper (medium, chopped)
- 1 green chili (small, diced)
- 2 scallions (chopped)
- 2 limes (juiced)
- ¼ cup fresh cilantro (chopped)

INSTRUCTIONS:
a) Preheat the oven to 400°F and spray cooking oil on a baking sheet.

b) Add chopped garlic into a processing machine with the beans, oats, chilli, and cornmeal. Add salt and pepper before processing the mixture.

c) Prepare a baking tray and spread the mixture on to it. Be sure to spray it with cooking oil before baking the mixture for 20 to 30 minutes.

d) before spraying it with more cooking oil and continue baking. This helps to ensure the whole mixture is baked evenly.

e) Once baked, take out the bean mixture in a bowl and mix it well with corn, bell pepper, chili and scallions.

f) The tortillas should be wrapped in foil and warmed in the oven for 5 minutes.

g) Spread the bean mixture on the tortillas and serve with corn salsa and cilantro topping.

85. Grilled Haloumi Tacos

Makes: 4

INGREDIENTS:

- Olive oil
- 2 husked ears of corn
- Kosher salt
- Black pepper
- 1 small, red onion, sliced
- $\frac{1}{2}$ kg halloumi, sliced into thick slices
- 8 corn tortillas

INSTRUCTIONS:

a) Prepare the grill setting it at medium-high heat and oil the grates thoroughly.

b) Lightly brush over the corn husks with oil and season the same with salt and pepper. Toss the onion rings with oil, salt, and pepper. Grill both the ingredients, 10-15 minutes for corn and 4 minutes for onions, turning often to make sure that it is tender, and is charred in spots.

c) Once the corn cools, cut the kernels from the cobs and place them in a medium bowl.

d) Brush the cheese with a little oil, and after seasoning with a little salt and pepper, grill it once on each side to char and warm completely.

e) Warm the tortillas in the microwave or on a cooler part of the grill to soften it.

f) Divide the cheese amongst the tortillas, topping them with onions, corn, avocado, cilantro, salsa and lime wedges.

86. The Simple Vegan Taco

Makes: 1

INGREDIENTS:
- 2 wheat tacos
- ½ cup black beans
- 1 avocado, sliced
- 2 cherry tomatoes, quartered
- 1 onion, chopped
- Fresh parsley
- Lime juice
- 1 Tablespoon olive
- oil
- Salt
- Your choice of hot sauce

INSTRUCTIONS:
a) Heat the taco to warm it thoroughly.

b) Place all the ingredients on the taco in any order you like. You can also heat up all the veggies in a medium skillet.

c) Simply heat the oil, add the onions, beans and cherry tomatoes and sprinkle a little salt over the whole.

d) Remove after one minute of constant stirring.

e) Serve the tacos, sprinkled with some parsley, sliced avocados, a splash of lime juice and the hot chili sauce to dip into.

87. Beans and Grilled Corn Taco

Makes: 2

INGREDIENTS:
- 2 Corn tacos
- $\frac{1}{2}$ cup black beans
- Grilled corn on the cob
- 1 avocado, sliced
- 2 cherry tomatoes, quartered
- 1 small onion, chopped
- Fresh parsley
- $\frac{1}{4}$ teaspoon cumin
- Salt
- Freshly ground black pepper
- 1 tablespoon Oil for grilling

INSTRUCTIONS:
a) Prepare the grill setting it at medium-high heat and oil the grates thoroughly.

b) Lightly brush over the corn husks with oil and season the same with salt and pepper. Grill the corn for 10-15 minutes turning often to make sure that it is tender, and charred in spots.

c) Once the corn cools, cut the kernels from the cobs and place them in a medium bowl.

d) Toss with black beans, sliced avocado, cherry tomatoes, chopped onions, fresh parsley and season with salt, black pepper, and cumin. Squeeze some fresh lime for a tangy filling.

e) Pile onto the taco and enjoy with a dip of your choice.

88. Black Beans and Rice Salad Taco

Makes: 4

INGREDIENTS:

- Taco shells
- 3 Lime, zest and juice
- 1 cup Cherry tomatoes, each cut into 4 pieces
- $\frac{1}{4}$ cup Red wine vinegar
- $\frac{1}{4}$ cup Red onion, small dice
- $\frac{1}{4}$ Cup Mixture of Cilantro, Basil and Scallions, all chiffonade
- 1 teaspoon Garlic, minced
- 1 can Corn, drained
- 1 Green chili pepper, small diced
- 1 Red, orange or yellow bell pepper
- 1 can Black beans, drained
- 1 $\frac{1}{2}$ Cup White rice, cooked and kept warm
- Salt and Pepper to season.

INSTRUCTIONS:

a) Cut the cherry tomatoes into quarters marinate with diced red onion, red wine vinegar, garlic and salt for 30 minutes.

b) Gather and prepare the peppers, herbs and limes. Combine them all together with the drained black beans and corn, and season well with salt and pepper.

c) Add the tomato mixture to the bean mixture. Then fold in the warm rice. Taste and add salt if needed.

d) Serve in taco shells.

89. Chewy Walnut Tacos

Makes: 4

INGREDIENTS:
TACO MEAT
- 1 cup raw walnuts
- 1 tablespoon yeast flakes
- 1 tablespoon of tamari
- ½ teaspoon ground cumin
- ¼ teaspoon chipotle pepper powder
- 1 teaspoon chili

FILLING
- 1 Hass avocado
- 1 Roma tomato, finely diced
- 6 tablespoons smoked cashew cheese dip
- 4 large lettuce leaves

INSTRUCTIONS:
TACO MEAT
a) Place walnuts, nutritional yeast, tamari, chili powder, cumin, and chipotle chili powder in a food processor and puree until the mixture resembles coarse crumbs.

FILLING
b) For toppings, place the avocado in a small bowl and mash with a fork until smooth. Stir in the tomato.

c) To assemble each taco, place a lettuce leaf on a cutting board, ribs side up. Place ¼ cup Walnut Taco Meat in the center of the sheet.

d) Top with 1½ tablespoons of the cashew cheese dip and a quarter of the avocado mixture.

90. Seitan Tacos

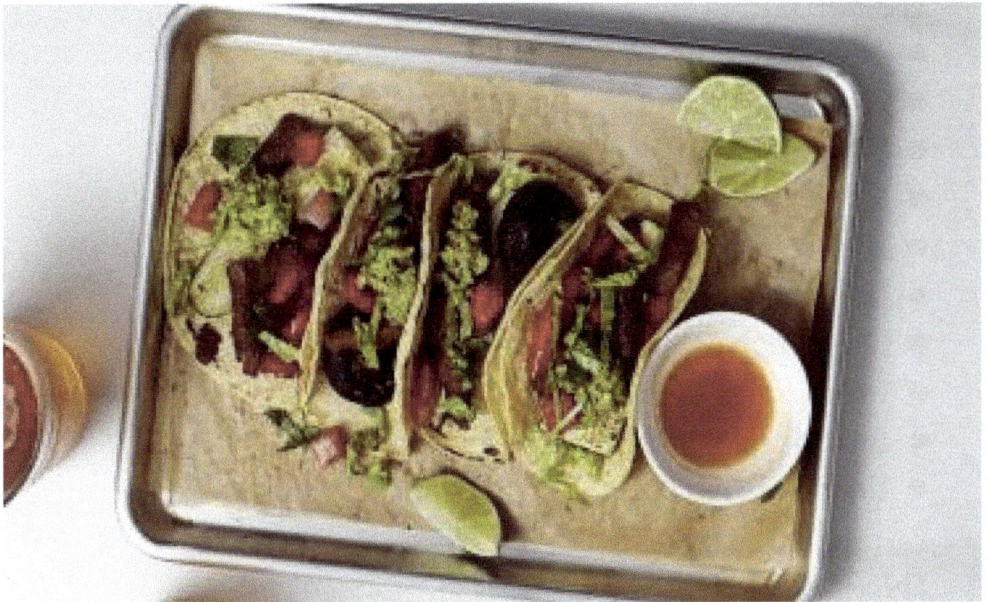

Makes: 4 tacos

INGREDIENTS:
- 2 tablespoons olive oil
- 12 ounces seitan
- 2 tablespoons soy sauce
- 11/2 teaspoons chili powder
- 1/4 teaspoon ground cumin
- 1/4 teaspoon garlic powder
- 12 (6-inch) soft corn tortillas
- 1 ripe Hass avocado
- Shredded romaine lettuce
- 1 cup tomato salsa

INSTRUCTIONS:
a) In a large skillet, heat the oil over medium heat. Add the seitan and cook until browned, about 10 minutes. Sprinkle with the soy sauce, chili powder, cumin, and garlic powder, stirring to coat. Remove from heat.
b) Preheat the oven to 225°F. In a medium skillet, warm the tortillas over medium heat and stack them on a heatproof plate. Cover with foil and place them in the oven to keep them soft and warm.
c) Pit and peel the avocado and cut into 1/4-inch slices.
d) Arrange the taco filling, avocado, and lettuce on a platter and serve along with the warmed tortillas, salsa, and any additional toppings.

91. Terrific tofu tacos

Makes: 6 servings

INGREDIENTS:
- 1 pounds Firm tofu; cut into $\frac{1}{2}$ inch cubes
- 2 tablespoons Red chile powder
- $\frac{1}{4}$ cup Vegetarian Worcestershire sauce
- Cooking spray
- $\frac{1}{2}$ Red onion; chopped
- $\frac{1}{4}$ cup Chopped cilantro
- 1 cup Shredded red cabbage
- 1 can Vegetarian refried black beans
- 12 Flour tortillas
- Salsa

INSTRUCTIONS:
a) In a large bowl, gently toss tofu with chile powder and Worcestershire sauce. Let stand for at least one hour. Preheat oven to 400 F. Lightly spray a baking sheet with cooking spray. Place tofu evenly across it.

b) Lightly spray top of tofu and bake for about 20 minutes until tofu is browned and slightly crispy. Remove from oven and let cool slightly. In a medium bowl, combine onion, cilantro, and cabbage.

c) Spread tortillas across 2 to 3 baking sheets so they barely overlap.

d) Smear center of each with about $1\frac{1}{2}$ tablespoons of beans and place in oven for about 10 minutes, until tortillas begin to brown and beans are hot.

e) Place equal amounts of tofu in center of each tortilla.

f) Top with onion-cabbage-cilantro mixture, fold in half, and place on a serving platter. Serve with salsa if desired.

92. Rajas con Crema Tacos

INGREDIENTS:
FILLING:
- 5 Poblano peppers, roasted, peeled, seeded, cut into strips
- ¼ Water
- 1 Onion, white, large, thinly sliced
- 2 cloves Garlic, minced
- ½ cup Vegetable stock or broth

CREMA:
- ½ cup Almonds, raw
- 1 clove Garlic
- ¾ cup Water
- ¼ cup Almond milk, unsweetened or vegetable oil
- 1 tablespoon Lemon juice fresh

INSTRUCTIONS:
a) Heat a large sauté pan to medium heat, add water. Add the onion and sweat for 2-3 minutes or until it is tender and translucent.

b) Add garlic, and ½ cup of vegetable stock, cover and let steam.

c) Add the Poblano peppers and let cook for 1 minute more. Season with salt and pepper. Remove from the heat and let cool slightly.

d) Place the almonds, garlic, water, almond milk, and lemon juice in the blender and process until smooth. Season with salt and pepper.

e) Pour the almond crema over the cooled filling and mix well.

93. Sweet Potato and Carrot Tinga Tacos

INGREDIENTS:

- ¼ cup Water
- 1 cup Thinly sliced white onion
- 3 Garlic cloves, minced
- 2 ½ cups Grated sweet potato
- 1 cup Grated carrot
- 1 can (14 ounces) Diced tomatoes
- 1 teaspoon Mexican oregano
- 2 Chipotle peppers in adobo
- ½ cup Vegetable stock
- 1 Avocado, sliced
- 8 Tortillas

INSTRUCTIONS:

a) In a large sauté pan over medium-heat, add water and onion, cook for 3 -4 minutes, until the onion is translucent and soft. Add the garlic and continue to cook, stirring for 1 minute.

b) Add sweet potato and carrot to the pan and cook for 5 min stirring often.

SAUCE:

c) Place the diced tomatoes, vegetable stock, oregano, and chipotle peppers in the blender and process until smooth.

d) Add chipotle-tomato sauce to the pan and cook for 10-12 minutes, stirring occasionally, until the sweet potatoes and carrot are cooked through. If necessary, add more vegetable stock to the pan.

e) Serve on warm tortillas and top with avocado slices.

94. Potato and Chorizo Tacos

Makes: 4 servings

INGREDIENTS:
- 1 tablespoon Vegetable oil, optional
- 1 cup Onion, white, minced
- 3 cups Potato, peeled, diced
- 1 cup Vegan chorizo, cooked
- 12 tortillas
- 1 cup Your favorite salsa

INSTRUCTIONS:
a) Heat 1 tablespoon of oil in a large sauté pan at medium-low heat. Add onions and cook until soft and translucent, about 10 minutes.

b) While the onions are cooking, place your cut potatoes in a small saucepot with salted water. Bring the water up to a simmer at high heat. Lower heat to medium and let the potatoes cook for 5 minutes.

c) Drain the potatoes and add them to the pan with the onion. Turn heat up to medium-high. Cook potatoes and onions for 5 minutes or until the potatoes begin to brown. Add more oil if necessary.

d) Add cooked chorizo to the pan and mix well. Cook for one more minute.

e) Season with salt and pepper.

f) Serve with warm tortillas and the salsa of your choice.

95. Summer Calabacitas Tacos

Makes: 4 servings

INGREDIENTS:
- $\frac{1}{2}$ cup Vegetable broth
- 1 cup Onion, white, finely diced
- 3 cloves Garlic, minced
- $\frac{1}{4}$ cup Vegetable stock or water
- 2 Zucchini, large, cut into dice
- 2 cups Tomato, diced
- 10 tortillas
- 1 Avocado, sliced
- 1 cup Favorite Salsa

INSTRUCTIONS:
a) In a large heavy bottomed pot, set to medium heat; sweat the onion in $\frac{1}{4}$ cup of vegetable broth for 2 to 3 minutes until onion is translucent.

b) Add garlic and pour in remaining $\frac{1}{4}$ cup of vegetable broth, cover and let steam.

c) Uncover, add zucchini and cook for 3-4 minutes, until it begins to soften.

d) Add tomato and cook for 5 minutes more, or until all the vegetables are tender.

e) Season to taste, and serve on warm tortillas with avocado slices and salsa.

96. Spicy Zucchini and Black Bean Tacos

Makes: 4 servings

INGREDIENTS:
- 1 tablespoon Vegetable oil, optional
- ½ White Onion, thinly sliced
- 3 cloves Garlic, minced
- 2 Mexican zucchini, large, diced
- 1 can (14.5 ounces) Black beans, drained

CHILE DE ARBOL SAUCE:
- 2 - 4 Chile de Arbol, dried
- 1 cup Almonds, raw
- ½ Onion, white, large
- 3 cloves Garlic, unpeeled
- 1 ½ cups Vegetable Stock, Warm

INSTRUCTIONS:
a) Heat vegetable oil to medium heat in a large sauté pan. Add onion and sweat for 2-3 minutes or until the onion is tender and translucent.

b) Add the garlic cloves and cook for 1 minute.

c) Add the zucchini and cook until tender, about 3-4 minutes. Add the black beans and mix well. Let cook for 1 minute more. Season with salt and pepper.

d) To make the sauce: heat a griddle, or cast iron pan to medium-high heat. Toast chiles on each side until lightly toasted, about 30 seconds on each side. Remove from pan and set aside.

e) Add the almonds to the pan and toast until golden, about 2 minutes. Remove from pan and set aside.

f) Toast the onion, and the garlic until slightly charred, about 4 minutes on each side.

g) Place the almonds, onion, garlic, and chiles in the blender. Add the warm vegetable stock. Process until smooth. Season with salt and pepper. Sauce should be thick and creamy.

97. Asparagus tacos

Makes: 1 serving

INGREDIENTS:
- 4 yellow corn tortillas
- 16 pieces asparagus, grilled
- $\frac{1}{4}$ cup Monterey jack cheese, shredded
- $\frac{1}{4}$ cup White Cheddar cheese, shredded
- Salt and pepper
- Olive oil, for brushing

INSTRUCTIONS:
a) Prepare grill.

b) For each taco, spread $\frac{1}{4}$ of the cheeses and 4 pieces of the asparagus on each tortilla, Season to taste with salt and pepper.

c) Fold in half. Brush the outside lightly with olive oil.

d) Grill for 3 minutes on each side or until tortilla is crispy and cheese has melted.

98. <u>Bean sprouts taco with beef</u>

Makes: 8 Servings

INGREDIENTS:
- 12 ounces Fuji bean sprouts
- 16 Taco shells
- $\frac{1}{4}$ Lettuce, shredded
- $\frac{1}{2}$ pack Taco seasoning mix (1.6 oz)
- 2 tablespoons Vegetable oil
- 1 Tomato, cubed
- 1 pounds Ground beef, cooked/drained

INSTRUCTIONS:
a) Stir-fry Fuji bean sprouts in oil over heat for 30 seconds.

b) Add beef prepared according to taco seasoning mix instructions.

c) Remove from heat, fill taco shells with desired amount of mixture, add tomato, lettuce and cheese.

99. Guacamole bean tacos

Makes: 1 serving

INGREDIENTS:
- 1 pack Taco shells
- 15 ounces Refried beans
- Guacamole
- Chopped onions
- Chopped tomatoes
- Shredded cheddar cheese

INSTRUCTIONS:
a) Heat taco shells in preheated 250 degrees oven until thoroughly heated, 5 minutes.

b) In small saucepan cook refried beans over low heat, stirring frequently, until heated thoroughly.

c) for each taco, spoon 2 rounded tablespoons each, beans and guacamole into a taco shell, sprinkle with onion, tomato and cheese.

d) May also add a little chopped lettuce.

100. Lentil tacos

Makes: 4 Servings

INGREDIENTS:

- 1 cup Onions; minced
- ½ cup Celery; minced
- 1 Clove garlic; minced
- 1 teaspoon Olive oil
- 1 cup Red lentils
- 1 tablespoon Chili powder
- 2 teaspoons Ground cumin
- 1 teaspoon Dried oregano
- 2 cups Chicken stock; defatted
- 2 tablespoons Raisins
- 1 cup Mild or spicy salsa
- 8 Corn tortillas
- Shredded lettuce
- Chopped tomatoes

INSTRUCTIONS:

a) In a large frying pan over medium heat, sauté the onions, celery and garlic in the oil for 5 minutes. Stir in the lentils, chili powder, cumin and oregano. Cook for 1 minutes. Add the stock and raisins. Cover and cook for 20 minutes, or until the lentils are tender.

b) Remove the lid and cook, stirring often, until the lentils are thickened, about 10 minutes. Stir in the salsa.

c) Wrap the tortillas in a damp paper towel and microwave on high for 1 minute, or until soft.

d) Divide the lentil mixture among the tortillas.

e) Top with the lettuce and tomatoes.

CONCLUSION

Tacos are a versatile and tasty meal that can be enjoyed by people of all ages. With their endless possibilities for fillings and toppings, they can be customized to suit anyone's taste preferences. From simple beef and cheese tacos to more elaborate vegetarian or seafood options, there is a taco recipe for everyone to enjoy. So next time you are in the mood for a quick and satisfying meal, consider making some delicious tacos and let your taste buds be delighted.

Ingram Content Group UK Ltd.
Milton Keynes UK
UKHW020612120623
423287UK00008B/42

9 781835 005590